Everyday Witchcraft

Everyday Witchcraft

Magic and Spells to Enchant a Modern Woman's Life

Kirsten Riddle

SPRING HILL

Published by Spring Hill

Spring Hill is an imprint of
How To Books Ltd
Spring Hill House
Spring Hill Road
Begbroke
Oxford
OX5 1RX
Tel: (01865) 375794
Fax: (01865) 379162

info@howtobooks.co.uk
www.howtobooks.co.uk

British Library Cataloguing in Publication Data
A catalogue record of this book is available from the British Library

ISBN13: 978-1-905862-12-2

Cover Design by Mousemat Design Ltd

Produced for How To Books by
Deer Park Productions, Tavistock
Designed and typeset by Mousemat Design Ltd
Printed and bound by Bell & Bain Ltd, Glasgow

NOTE: The material contained in this book is set out in good faith
for general guidance and no liability can be accepted for loss or
expense incurred as a result of relying in particular circumstances on
statements made in the book. Laws and regulations are complex and
liable to change, and readers should check the current position with
relevant authorities before making personal arrangements.

Contents

Introduction   7
     And so it begins...   7
     What *is* magic?   7
     Enchanting your life   10

PART 1: MAGIC AND WITCHCRAFT   13
Chapter 1: Magical beginnings   14
     The history of witchcraft   14
     Finding the balance in life   16
     Witchcraft: good or bad?   17
     It started with a wish: magic and you   18
     Invoking your Inner Goddess   21

Chapter 2: Preparation for witchcraft   26
     Magical spaces, personal power spots and altars   26
     Protection techniques   29

Chapter 3: Casting spells   32
     Putting a bit of magic into your life   32
     The Seasons   41

Chapter 4: A house witch's store cupboard   44
     Some rules and thoughts on spell-casting   44
     Using everyday ingredients in magic   45
     Magical tools   56

Chapter 5: Enchanting associates   60
     Inventing your magical self   60
     Making friends in high places   69

PART 2: SPELLS   73
Chapter 6: Spells for love, relationships and sex   74
   Spells for drawing love and affection   77
   Spells for keeping love strong   81
   Spells for marriage and divorce   85
   Spells for sex and fertility   87

Chapter 7: Spells for money, good fortune and success   92

Chapter 8: Spells for work and career   102

Chapter 9: Spells for home and family   107

Chapter 10: Spells for health and well-being   113

Chapter 11: Spells for power, psychic development and protection   122
   Spells for power   123
   Spells for psychic development   128
   Spells for protecting you and your home   130

Chapter 12: Spells on the move   136
   Handbag magic   137
   Cyber magic   144

Chapter 13: Spells for sleeping and dreaming   147
   Tips for a good night's sleep   148
   Spells to encourage dreams   151
   Tips to prevent nightmares   158

Chapter 14: Magic and the environment   160
   Healing yourself, the world and the washing machine   161
   Magical interiors   162
   More advanced magical tools   168
   Witchy words of wisdom   173

Bibliography and further reading   175

Introduction

And so it begins...

Do you fancy bringing a little magic into your life? I'm guessing the answer is yes, or you wouldn't be reading this book! The first question that usually springs to mind on the subject of magic is, 'Does it work?' My answer is, 'Try it and see.' The second question is, '*How* does it work?' How can something which seems better suited to a fantasy book have any real effect on our lives? The truth is magic is a force that has visible results. It happens on so many different levels. Sometimes the effects are obvious; sometimes it takes a little time and understanding for things to become clear. One thing is certain – you don't need special powers akin to a witch or a superhero to make a magical difference.

What is magic?

Magic is all around us. It's in the beauty of our environment whether it's a lush country landscape or an urban mishmash of bricks and concrete. It's in the smile of a stranger that touches your heart; the wish made on a starry night; or the prayer for hope and healing said before we slip into sleep. Magic is the natural energy that moves within us and around us. We can tap into this force any time we like and use it to improve our circumstances and those of others.

Modern magic

There's no need to adorn a black cloak and pointy hat and dance under a full Moon to achieve your aims – although it could be a fun experience! Magic has changed over the centuries; witches are no longer the warty-nosed hags of fairy tales. The 21st-century enchantress is a sexy sorceress who feels more at home in the meeting room or the supermarket than toiling over a bubbling cauldron with her eye of newt. She knows that working the right spell takes a dollop of intent, a knack for seeing the magical in the ordinary, and a little imagination, along with a basic knowledge of special ingredients.

Magic is about attitude. It's about making the best of your innate abilities and contacting your Inner Goddess (yes, you really do have one and she's raring to break free!). It's about self-esteem and understanding. It's about empathising with situations and people, because it's only when you're intuitively primed that you come up with the best magical solution to a problem. Most importantly magic is about positive change.

Cooking up spells

Spells are a way of focusing the will to bring about a positive effect. Broomsticks, cauldrons and magic wands are not necessary; though that's not to say that they don't have their uses. Broomsticks clear away clutter and the act of brushing is a great way to cleanse an area of negative vibrations (as well as dust!). Cauldrons are wonderful for cooking up all manner of lotions and potions without soiling a cooking pot, and wands make excellent tools for directing your wishes as well as being interesting ornaments and great talking pieces at parties!

When you cast a spell, you are, in effect, making a wish. All it requires is the belief that things will happen, followed by an action to substantiate this. Think about a birthday wish. The cake is presented, the candles lit. Now it's up to you to focus on the one thing you would like. You visualise it in your mind. You see it and feel what it would be like to have it in your life. Then with a deep breath you focus that intention as you blow out the flames. You can't know for certain that your wish will be granted, but you still believe in it because it's tradition, it's part of that special birthday magic.

Spells are not about fancy ingredients. You don't have to go far to find the things you need; most likely you already have them in your kitchen cupboard or garden; if not, a trip to the shops will soon have your witchy cupboards groaning.

Everything in this world has a magical vibration (including you!). The key to a successful spell is finding the right ingredients and being able to visualise what you want in a clear and focused manner.

Spells can be performed in a number of ways. You can make lotions or potions, burn candles, or take specially scented herbal baths; you can use visualisation with a few choice words to create spells on the move: it doesn't matter which method you choose. The more personal you make the spell, the more likely it is to work for you.

Creating a spell is like cooking a wonderful meal. First you must think about what you want from it. Are you looking for something quick and filling that will keep you going through the day? Maybe you want something to amaze and delight your taste buds. Or perhaps you're looking for something special and substantial that will nourish you and get you firing on all cylinders. You will approach the cooking in different ways depending on your needs and limitations.

Next you need to consider what to include. If you haven't much time, choose ingredients that are simple to prepare and quick to cook. If you have all afternoon, you may want to immerse yourself in preparation, and really go to town on your meal. It depends on how you feel and what you have available. You will also have to consider what you *fancy* eating. We all have tastes that change from day to day, and just as you might feel the urge for a particular food; you might also feel drawn towards a particular ingredient for a spell. Trust your intuition!

Finally you will invest love and energy in your meal. As you're cooking, you might be imagining how the meal will taste, what it might look like on the plate and how you're going to feel eating it. The same can be said for casting a spell. As you mix the ingredients together, you will focus on your intention, you will picture what it is you want and see yourself achieving this.

Everyone can cook a meal, even something simple like heating up a can of soup, and so everyone can perform magic if they adopt a similar approach. You don't need cupboards full of strange ingredients for magic to work. The ritual of preparation and the intention of your will is enough for an effective spell. You'd be surprised at how many items on your shopping list have magical properties. Look in your fridge – milk, cheese, eggs can all be used in spells. Bread and rice, two food essentials, are excellent for drawing money and prosperity into the home. Apples have been used for centuries in love magic. Staple kitchen herbs like basil, sage and rosemary have numerous magical properties.

Enchanting your life

In this book you will find a wealth of simple exercises and suggestions to help make your life more enchanting. There are tips on types of spells best suited to busy lives, and ingredients to help you in your magical quest. Whether you want to increase your good fortune, or attract a soul mate, make a stunning first impression, or find a parking space, the power is at your fingertips.

You will find that once you begin tapping into this inner force everything falls into place. Positive coincidences increase and you will start to notice the magic that is all around you. Trust your instincts. Trust yourself as a magical woman and let the enchantment begin.

Part One
Magic and witchcraft

Part 1 of this book looks at magic and witchcraft: what witchcraft is and how it began, what you can use it for and what you might need to make it work. You will discover the tools you have at your fingertips and how to use them to transform your life magically. You will learn the importance of the planets and the seasons, and the types of spell and when to perform them. You will learn simple techniques to protect and prepare yourself. This part of the book focuses on the how and why, giving you the grounding you need to put your magic into action.

CHAPTER ONE

Magical Beginnings

The History of Witchcraft

Witchcraft is old! In Britain, its roots are pre-Christian, in the time of the pagans. The word conjures up images of ancient mystics living in caves and bubbling up potions in stone pots – and that might not be too far from the truth! The word itself means 'craft of the wise', and that's exactly what it is; a craft, an art form carried out by those who have the knowledge.

The word *witch* has its origins in the Anglo-Saxon word *wicce*, which means *wise*. The root of this is *wic* which means *bend or twist* (and gives rise to the noun *Wicca*), and this is just what a witch does. Witches use magic to bend and twist natural energies in order to effect a change.

Some say Wicca is a religion, and that is true, those who practise witchcraft and choose this path do consider it a religion. They call themselves Wiccans, and they worship the old ways, the god and the goddess in any number of forms. Others say it is simply something they choose to do, a way to help themselves and others, a tradition. Witchcraft can be either of these things. It is a way of life, and there are certain rules and regulations, but these are not meant to be restrictive; far from it, these rules are in place to help those who practise get the best out of their craft.

Witchcraft exists around the world, and has done for centuries in many different guises. In the past it has been associated with devil worship and Satanism and witches have been depicted as evil-doers who use magic to harm others. Folklore is littered with tales of witches and their despicable acts; it was commonly thought that they were in league with the devil. This superstitious belief was introduced by the Church to demonise witchcraft, and turn people against its ways. Interestingly, in Wicca there is no such thing as the devil: he doesn't exist. The Church introduced him as a scare tactic!

During the witch trials (particularly in the 14th century), innocent women were persecuted just for behaving or looking differently, for having healing knowledge or for being of a certain age and living alone. Death, disease and misfortune were all blamed on the lowly witch. Ironically, the accusers were giving witchcraft far more power than seems possible. Their allegations were based on fear and ignorance, just as any prejudice is.

The Wicca of today is an amalgamation of pagan, folk and magical rites from around the world. There are influences from far-flung mythologies, including Egyptian, Celtic, Greek, Roman and Babylonian. Today's witches have the freedom to explore and decide for themselves which bits of folklore and practice to incorporate into their magical work. This might sound like a pick-and-mix way to operate, but witchcraft is not set in stone, it takes a fluid path. It allows its followers the freedom to experiment and find out what works for them. This is the beauty of the craft.

Finding the balance in life

One element of witchcraft that remains unchanged is that of duality, the yin and yang balance of Wicca. Witchcraft is about finding the right balance in all things. To do this we need both the masculine and feminine energies: men may seem to be from Mars and women from Venus, but the reality is that we complement each other, and what may appear to be extreme differences can and do work in our favour.

Just as the seasons dip and change, so do we as individuals, and so does our life cycle. Witches understand this and they work with these fluctuating energies, both in nature and within themselves. Think about the Moon and the myriad of changes it goes through every month. During its waxing period (the phase where it grows to a full Moon) it is building up to action, and in magical terms drawing things to us. This phase relates to those masculine energies. During its waning period (where it reduces in size) it is calming down, soothing and letting go. This is its feminine phase. Each phase of the Moon is equally as important, because without one we would not have the other. The Moon has to travel the full cycle every month to reach where it is supposed to be, just as we, in our lives, have times of frenetic action and then quieter times when we must recharge our batteries. This is the law of nature.

Witches worship the god and goddess of Wicca, or lord and lady as they are often called. Both sides of the spiritual coin are equally as important. The goddess is nurturing, caring and gentle; the god is assertive, full of action and energy.

Elements of the god and goddess are often drawn from

mythology. Witches can and do work with a number of different deities, depending on their magical requirements, because they are all part of the same thing: the universal male and female energy. So, if a witch wanted to work a spell for fertility, she might look for a particular goddess whose prime association is fertility. She would have lots to choose from!

Witches believe that the god and goddess are not unseen beings to be revered from a distance. They exist in heart and mind, they exist in nature, and their influence can be seen and felt everywhere.

Witchcraft: good or bad?

As a witch you can choose to follow the craft as a religion or simply a part of life and something that you incorporate into your daily routine. You can choose to shout your beliefs from the rooftops, or keep them quiet. At the end of the day, witchcraft is flexible and can be adapted to fit you.

Many experienced and adept witches hold down 'conventional' careers and positions of power. Not all of them make it common knowledge that they practise magic. Even today, there are still those who are nervous of the words *magic* and *witch*, so sometimes it is easier to keep your views private, or introduce people to the craft gradually, showing rather than telling them what it is about. Having said that, witchcraft is not a flight of fancy made up of whimsical tales and superstition; it is a belief system, a way of life that includes practising magic to benefit all.

Witchcraft is empowering, and many women practise magic to bring about positive change and to encourage spiritual growth. The days of wicked witches and evil sorcery are long gone. That's not to say that it isn't possible to inflict revenge and damage through spells;

it is. But it is less about dark magic and more about a person's true nature. As with anything, the choice is down to the individual. Like attracts like: if you think 'evil' thoughts, you will create a bad atmosphere and attract those of a similar nature; if you think happy thoughts, you will attract happy, positive people.

Think about it for a moment. We've all had days when everything seems to go wrong – it starts with an isolated incident that puts us in bad mood, and then it's like a roller-coaster of disasters building up speed as the day progresses. By the same token, if something puts us in a good mood from early on, we are almost certain to have a brilliant day with lots of happy occurrences and a constant smile on our faces. Our mindset on each of these days has much to do with the way we see things: setbacks become problems rather than enjoyable challenges.

Witchcraft does not allow you to blame your actions on outside influences. You are responsible for everything you do, every thought and every action. This might sound a heavy burden, but in fact it is liberating; because if you are responsible for the things that happen in your life, you also have the power to change them!

It started with a wish: magic and you

So now you know a little about the history of the craft, we come to the important question that witches are asked over and over again: 'What is magic?' It's not about hocus-pocus and elaborate theatrics, and it certainly doesn't involve the manipulation of others, as many supernatural films would have us believe. Magic is less 'Hollywood' than 'local wood' and being in tune with nature. Any witch worth her Wicca salt will tell you that magic is not like it is in the movies. It's earthy, solid, warm and real and it's a power that can be used by anyone to achieve a positive outcome.

Magic is in everyone and everything. Every living item has an energy field, a magical vibration which can be used in spells. To know about magic, you have to know about yourself and the world around you. You have to go back to your primeval instincts. To perform magic you have to employ a sixth sense and learn to trust your intuition, because the best magic is that which you create yourself when you are in tune with your magical aims.

There are three simple steps to making magic work for you. Once you have mastered these you will be able to create spells to suit your needs; spells that have your own individual stamp on them.

Step 1: Understand your intention

Like anything in life, magic requires that we have a very specific intention. We must know what we want. If we don't, the magic will be sketchy, there will be no real direction to it. Magical energies are powerful, and unless you can define exactly what you want the outcome of your spell to be, you might find that the results are not what you expected. This is because you didn't have a clear picture in your mind.

So, before putting any spell into practice, be sure that you know *exactly* what you want to achieve. Spend time thinking about your magical aim. Examine your motives. Why do you want this so much? What will it change for you or those around you? It's always wise to look at why you want something, what the underlying need is and whether it is moral and fair. Will getting what you want affect anyone else in a negative way? That's an important question to ask before any spell.

Once you have decided on your intention, keep it clearly in your mind as you prepare for your spell and during any ritual that you might use. Visualise your intention as clearly as possible. Visualisation is the key to magical success. The ability to picture things in your head is a skill that takes practice but can greatly improve any magical results.

Improve your visualisation skills

Take a piece of fruit. Find a quiet, comfortable place to sit where you won't be disturbed. Place the fruit in front of you so you can see it clearly. Look at it for a few minutes. Really look at it, noticing the shape and texture, the colour, any unusual marks or indentations.

Now close your eyes and recall the fruit to your mind. See it as clearly as you can, remember all the little things you noticed. Hold the picture for as long as you can.

Now imagine that you are reaching out and picking up the fruit. How does it feel in your hand? Bring it to your lips. Smell it. Take a bite. What does it taste like? Do you like the taste? Consider the fruit with all your senses.

Once you have done this, open your eyes and just look at the fruit again. How does the picture in your head match the real thing?

This exercise can be done with any object. The benefit of using something edible is that you can involve all your senses. The more comprehensive your visualisation is, the more likely it will bring results, so learn to picture things as fully as possible. Engage your feelings, because emotion plays a very important part in magic.

Step 2: Believe in yourself

It may sound a simple thing to do, but it's amazing how many people in the world today lack self-belief. To achieve anything in life, you have to first of all *believe* that you can do it. If you don't have any belief in yourself, how can you hope to reach your goals, and how can you convince others that they are achievable?

Belief, like most things, does tend to waver; it comes and goes depending on the mood and situation, but in magic you have to have 100 per cent faith that your spell has worked. There must be no doubt in your mind as you carry out the spell and afterwards, no lingering worries or fears. Once you have performed the spell, be confident that it has worked. Have confidence in your abilities. Like attracts like, so if you have an air of confidence and a self assured and positive energy about you, you will attract similar energies from the Universe.

Step 3: Perform the ritual

In magic we use the word *ritual* to describe the various aspects of performing a spell: the things we do (lighting candles, anointing, burning herbs and so on), and the words we say. In a ritual, what you do is not as important as the 'doing' of it. Consider something as simple as lighting a candle. The act of lighting the candle focuses your mind on the intention, it strengthens your belief in the magic. It acts as a catalyst for the energies around you to work.

Rituals can be very complex, involving ceremonies to worship the goddess, and long and complicated chants and invocations. These ornate rituals are no more powerful than the simple act of brewing a special magical tea and saying a few words as it simmers away. The act of choosing the herbs to match your aim, the act of boiling them in a pot while visualising your goal is all part of the ritual and just another way of focusing your mind and acknowledging your need.

Invoking your Inner Goddess

This might sound a little far-fetched and supernatural, but it's actually something most women have done at some time or other without realising it. Remember that last special night out you planned, that event where you wanted to sparkle and be admired by all and sundry. What do we do on those occasions? We pamper and preen in the mirror, we give ourselves admiring glances, imagine that we are a film star or fashion icon. We put ourselves on a pedestal in the hope that others will keep us there. In effect, we are invoking our Inner Goddess. We are releasing an alter ego, a part of ourselves that resides inside and very rarely sees the light of day. It's that part of ourselves that we need to tap into to let our real power shine. It's our femininity, our nurturing nature that links us to the Wicca goddess, to Mother Nature, and to all things.

In medieval times, women were often considered to be at their most powerful during menstruation. Women were the givers of life. They could bleed for several days, and yet they still lived; how could this be? The very fact that this happened was considered witchcraft. Menstrual blood was deemed the most powerful magical ingredient in existence. If used in spells, it gave the spell caster complete control over others and the ability to bend wills. Even now there are spells (most often to do with love and domination) that advocate the use of menstrual blood. I would not recommend using these spells. They are not very pleasant! And they are linked with manipulation and control of others, something that true magic and witchcraft does not support. However, it is interesting to note that women were seen as a threat simply because of their femininity. Today's society views things very differently, and many women hold positions of great power and are treated with the respect they deserve.

Invoking your Inner Goddess is about remembering, accepting and encouraging your true nurturing (and absolutely fabulous!) nature.

Access your Inner Goddess

Find a quiet space where you will not be disturbed. Sit with your back straight and your shoulders relaxed. Light some candles and burn some relaxing oils (lavender and bergamot essential oils are good for this).

Close your eyes and focus on your breathing. Take a long, slow, deep breath in and as you do so, imagine that you are breathing in light and love from the universe. As you breathe out, imagine that you are purging your body of any negative energies, pouring out all the stresses and strains of your life. Continue to do this until you feel completely relaxed.

When you are ready, imagine a door. It can be any kind of door – elaborate, ornate, wooden... Remember, the more detail you can give the image, the easier it will be to fix in your mind. This door opens into your subconscious. When you have a clear image in your mind, step towards the door, open it, walk through and close the door behind you.

Take a few moments to look at your surroundings. You are in a large room with high walls and windows. Look at the walls: are there any pictures on them? What about furniture? Is there anything on the floor: rugs, carpet, stone? Make sure you build up a clear picture of the room and its contents.

It is at this point that you notice a mirror in the far corner of the room. It is large and golden and there are strange swirling shadows on its surface. This is a magical mirror. This mirror is going to introduce you to your Inner Goddess.

When you are ready, move towards the mirror until you are standing before it. Now look at your reflection. You look different. You recognise yourself, but there is something enchanting about your appearance. Perhaps you are wearing different clothes. Maybe your hair is a different style. There is a shine, an inner glow that makes your skin gleam and your eyes sparkle. Take a moment to admire your reflection. This is you at your most magical. This is the wonderful nurturing part of you that connects with the Goddess and makes your magic work. Notice how you feel, and any impressions that come to you. Perhaps your mirror image has a message for you. Use this time to find things out and ask questions.

When you are ready, turn away from the mirror and move back to the door. Open it and return to the still of your mind, bringing with you the lovely image of your Inner Goddess and anything you may have learned. Focus on your breathing once more and when you are ready, open your eyes.

As with any visualisation in this book, it is always helpful to make notes afterwards. Images and messages come to us at all times so be sure to write down everything you can remember, including how you felt during and after the exercise. The more you perform this visualisation the more confident and powerful you will feel. It will become easier for you to access your Inner Goddess at any time, just by recalling the images and feelings. You can carry out this visualisation before performing spells and make it part of your magical preparation.

Other visualisation exercises

The more you visualise, the easier it becomes. So try the following exercises as often as you can. They can be done as you go about your daily business. In fact, the more you attempt to visualise as you work and play, the more effortless it becomes, until you can project magic and conjure spells at the drop of a hat!

Friendly vibes

Think of a close friend or family member. Really see them in your mind's eye. Explore their face, their expression. What are they wearing? How are they standing? Try to hold the image in your mind for as long as possible. Now imagine sending a ball of loving energy to this person. See it projecting from the middle of your forehead and hitting them gently in the face. See the energy explode into thousands of dancing lights that surround the person. See them smile as they receive these wonderful loving vibes.

You can do this exercise to heal or help anyone in need. Interestingly, after performing this visualisation you may often get a call or some kind of contact from the person you have been thinking about.

Thinking ahead

As you go about your daily routine, there will be certain activities that you do every day, whether it's picking the children up from school, travelling to work, or having a family meal together. Think about a forthcoming activity. Picture the scene in your head and how you would like it to go. Experience the feelings that you want to feel at that time. For instance, if you're having a family meal, you might want it to be an easy, relaxing, fun time, with everyone chatting about their day. See this and feel it. Surround this image with bright white light to seal it in your mind. Then carry on as normal.

This kind of implantation technique can be used in a number of situations when you want to achieve something positive, for example an exam, interview or performance.

★★★ CHAPTER TWO ★★★
Preparation for witchcraft

Magical spaces, personal power spots and altars ★★

Most witches practise various techniques to prepare themselves before they conduct any magical rituals. Sometimes these routines involve personal cleansing and preparation; sometimes they include clearing a sacred space where they can perform the magic to the best of their abilities. This second activity is called *casting a circle*.

The act of casting a circle clears a space of negative energies, and provides a safe area for you to perform your spell and raise magical power. It concentrates the power behind the spell and helps to focus intention. Of course, there are many situations where it is not possible to cast a circle due to time and circumstance: magic on the move, in the office and so on. However, certain visualisation techniques can be used to cleanse a space and give you the best working environment for your spells.

Casting a circle can be as elaborate or as simple you wish. Below, I suggest a mix of visualisation and the physical marking out of the directions to support this. Once you have tried this a few times, you will probably find that you don't have to mark out the circle physically, as you can see it easily in your mind's eye. This is the point at which you are ready to take your magic on the move!

Casting a circle

The first time you do this, to help with your visualisation, gather some stones and candles together. You can use crystals, or pebbles from your garden – they work equally well. Take four candles. Place one in front of you, one behind and one each to the left and right of you and then light them. Next take the stones and begin to mark out a circle around you.

Now visualise a shower of white light pouring down from the sky. This is a sacred light filled with loving energy. As it hits the top of your head, imagine it spilling out into the circle you have created. See yourself sitting in a circle of bright white light descending from the heavens. You may choose to say a few words at this point, something like: *I cast this circle of light, to aid me in my magical plight. May this space be filled with love and grace. Protect me and keep me safe.*

You may also want to invite the Goddess to join you in the circle. All you need to do is ask for her blessing in your magical work. Ask her to watch over you as you perform your spell. You may want to visualise her in the circle with you, or simply be aware of her loving, nurturing energy around you.

Casting a circle is as individual as any ritual or spell that you perform. The key is to do what feels right to you. The most important thing to remember is that the circle is a special place for you to raise your magic, a place where you can feel safe.

The coffee-table altar

Yes, you did read that correctly! An altar can be made of anything; the smallest, oldest table can become a magical altar if you want it to be. The idea behind the altar is that it is a place where you worship the Goddess, or a particular magical deity, or cause. In other words, you can build an altar to anything.

Many spells require that you build some sort of altar that focuses on your desired outcome. For instance, I have known fertility spells which suggest building a baby altar, and placing upon it various herbs associated with fertility, pictures of babies, and anything that you would associate with childbirth. Love altars can be created by placing a vase of pink roses and a piece of rose quartz along with various ornamental hearts upon a coffee table cleared for that purpose.

Altars can be changed on a daily basis to suit your needs. Many witches will ensure that the same key elements are always in place: a *pentacle*, a *wand*, a *cup* and an *athame* (a magical dagger) – these four items represent the elements earth, air, water and fire. However, this is not always appropriate, particularly for modern women on the move, who want to keep their magical practices private.

To simplify things, why not use your coffee table as a permanent altar and add items on a daily basis or at the time of your magical work? Fresh flowers are always good to place on an altar; they celebrate the living, nurturing aspects of witchcraft. Stones and crystals are also worth including, and statues and candles that support your aims.

I have known witches carry mobile altars with them, but I doubt you could fit all the items in your handbag! There are already so many essential magical accessories (such as lipstick, mascara, mirror, comb and perfume) to carry with us, it's best not to add to that burden. Incidentally, all of the above can be charged magically, and you can even make your own power oil to carry about in your purse for those occasions when you need a bit of a boost. More of that later…

Protection techniques

When you want to perform a spell, you are opening yourself up to the energies of the universe, so it's a good idea to employ some protection techniques.

As humans we all have an aura; this is like a field of energy surrounding our physical bodies, like the children in those old Ready Brek adverts! The aura can be affected by many things; if we are under the weather or emotionally drained, this will show in our aura. Many skilled psychics can actually see the aura; they can see the different colours and have learned to associate meanings with this. The opening up involved in magic can affect our auras, and we may feel tired and drained.

So, it's always a good idea to perform a quick protection ritual before doing any spell. The following techniques can be carried out anywhere. You can also use them at any point in your daily routine when you feel under threat or insecure.

The psychic egg

This is one of the most effective techniques for protection and can be done at any time. (It will also come up later in Chapter 12: Spells on the move.)

All you need to do is visualise yourself surrounded by bright golden light in the form of an egg or sphere. The light is like a shell; it protects you from outside influences. Any negative energy that comes your way will be bounced back.

Going back to your roots

Earthing is another valuable technique to perform both before and after a magic spell. It's very easy and helps to balance emotions.

Place your feet flat on the floor. Now imagine roots stretching from the soles of your feet into the ground. Imagine them reaching further and further until they are deep beneath the surface, sinking into the rich vibrant soil. Feel the energy of the Earth in your feet. Let the weight of your body sink down into your feet, through your skin and into the Earth. Anchor yourself for a minute. Take some deep breaths and know that you are balanced and supported by Mother Earth.

Flying

Just as you can anchor yourself to the Earth, you can also send your spirit soaring and give any spells a magical surge of energy with this 'flying' technique. It's also a fun activity, although be aware that afterwards you might feel a little light-headed, so be sure to have a drink of water at hand and, if you still feel giddy, practise the above earthing technique.

Performing this visualisation can have startling results. It's uncanny the number of times an unexpected surprise lands on the doorstep after you've been flying through the stars.

Flying

Stand with your feet shoulder-width apart. Make sure you feel comfortable and relaxed. Breathe deeply. Focus your attention on the area just above the navel and below the breastbone – the solar plexus. Imagine a ball of bright white energy burning inside you. This energy is the core essence of your being. Feel it burning, feel the warmth inside your chest. Focus all your attention on this, until you can no longer feel your arms and legs, until all your awareness resides in this part of your body.

Now see that ball of energy rising up through your chest, up through your neck and face until it bursts out the top of your head. As this happens, let it take your attention with it. You are now that ball of light flying high. Hover for a moment, and look down upon yourself.

When you are ready, send your attention soaring. Imagine that you can travel through walls and ceilings, that you are a shooting star climbing through the sky, and buildings below you become smaller and smaller until you are sailing above the clouds, until you can no longer see your house, or city; you are soaring towards the cosmos, dancing with the stars.

When you are ready, and this could happen quite fast as it's a difficult visualisation to hold onto for long, slowly bring yourself down to Earth. Travel past the clouds until you sink back through the ceiling, back into your room, back into your body, and once more return your attention to the energy within your solar plexus.

This is a wonderful visualisation to perform when you are feeling jaded. It helps you to realise that the world is an amazing place, that we are all part of a wonderful and vibrant universe.

You can use this technique in magic after you have performed your spell, to support your intentions. As you soar out of your body and up into the universe, keep in mind the outcome of the spell. Think of a phrase which sums up your intentions. When you reach the stars in your visualisation, stop for a moment and repeat the phrase. Remember to keep it in the present tense, not the future, as this only puts the outcome in the future. So, for instance, if you are looking for a new job, you might say, 'I now have the perfect job for me.'

★★★CHAPTER THREE★★★
Casting spells

Putting a bit of magic in your life

Magic is a word that covers a broad spectrum of things. In witchcraft, there are as many different types of magic as there are different types of witches. Generally speaking, magic is flexible. Witchcraft doesn't have to be performed in a coven to work – although if you'd like to get a group of like-minded friends together for a girly evening of light-hearted spell work, that's fine! It doesn't have to involve bubbling cauldrons or specific chants, unless you've always fancied yourself as a mystic crone!

I can't stress enough the importance of tailoring magic to suit your needs and lifestyle. This is what this book is all about. It's about finding the best path for you, in effect the path of least resistance, so that you can use magic to bring about positive change, without having to alter your life dramatically for a spell to work. The world is full of busy people. Modern women are continually having to juggle work, family, friends, relationships; there are so many balls to keep in the air, it's no wonder the pressure gets to us. For magic to make a significant difference, it has to be easily incorporated into our lives.

There are many different types of spell that you can use, and each one fits into one of two categories: spells that work on an internal level (teas, infusions, lotions, potions and magical baths), and spells that work externally (charms, amulets, talismans and candle magic).

Internal spells work upon you and how you feel. They will change you from the inside out so that you attract the things you need. External spells generate their own energy to draw things to you and bring about change. For example, if you want to soothe your broken heart, your best spell is one that works on you internally, something that's going to lift your spirits. If, however, you want to draw a new love into your life, you'd be better suited to a spell that works on an external level to attract things to you.

Spells that work on the inside

Strictly speaking, all spells work on and in you, because all your spells come from the power within you. All spells are blessed by your will and intention and also the belief you have in yourself. However, the particular process of *affecting you internally* is how certain types of spell will bring your desired outcome.

Teas, infusions, lotions and potions

It is fairly obvious to suggest that what you put into your body will have an effect on you, and this also goes for any magical foods or drinks you prepare.

Teas and infusions are very common in magic and have been used for centuries. You may think that PG Tips or Typhoo is all you need to know when it comes to making a good brew, but there are some lovely herbal teas that can be made very simply by boiling the kettle and stewing various herbs in the water. Tea strainers (available from most kitchenware shops) are ideal for this purpose.

Broths and stews have also been around for a long while and can be likened to magical potions, made from boiling various herbs in different liquids.

Poultices can be made up using herbs wrapped in fabric, and creams and lotions are often applied to skin as part of a magical ritual or for their healing properties.

Dream pillows

Little dream pillows or sachets are very common, and are easy to make from sections of material sewn together and filled with selected herbs and oils. These pillows can then be placed under a normal pillow to induce dreams or psychic messages in sleep. The choice of herbs and oils is very important, as it is their energies and scents that will relax you and help you to tune into your subconscious mind while sleeping.

Magical baths

Most people would agree that a bath can be a magical experience, but magical baths work on many different levels and can be very powerful spells. A magical bath requires various ingredients to be added to your bath water as part of the spell. The ingredients might be an infusion poured directly in the bath, or they can be held in muslin sachets so they don't scatter and clog up the plug hole. Even the act of adding a few drops of essential oil can be considered magical if carried out with enough focus and intent.

Spells that work on the outside

Again, just as all spells work on you, so too do all spells have an influence on your external circumstances, because if you change something in yourself, it affects how you see the world and more importantly how the world sees you. Spells that focus directly on external circumstances and effecting change are very powerful spells because they work with outside influences.

Candle magic

Candle magic is particularly effective as it involves the element of fire. It is also easy to perform. Candles come in all shapes, sizes and colours. If in doubt where to start, pick a church-style candle in a colour that matches your magical aim (every colour has a different significance).

Candle magic can be as simple as lighting a candle and visualising the outcome you would like. It can also involve anointing the candle with specific oils before you light it. This means rubbing the candle in the oil while focusing on your desires. Some spells suggest inscribing the candle with words or symbols. This can be done with a pin, or even a pen or pencil in some cases. Other spells suggest writing your magical intention on a piece of paper and then burning it in the anointed candle. There are many variations, and it's up to you which you choose for your spells. Always remember to let the candle burn out; this may take several consecutive days of performing the same spell.

You can also buy specially crafted candles. For example, candles in the shape of two people entwined are ideal for love spells. Red and black candles in the shape of a witch can be used in protection spells, and rainbow-coloured candles are very powerful and can be used to bring good fortune into your life.

Colour associations for candles

White: purification, cleansing, Moon spells, creativity

Pink: love and romance

Red: love, lust, passion, sex, fertility, assertiveness

Green: money, prosperity, success, growth, healing

Blue: healing, protection

Purple: power, psychic development

Yellow/gold: friendship, success, glory, fame

Brown: balance and grounding

Black: protection, breaking curses, banishing negativity

Charms, amulets and talismans

Charms, amulets and talismans are often confused in magic, as they do similar jobs, but there are differences. The one thing they *do* have in common is that each one is either worn or carried about the person in order to fulfil a particular need. That need could be protection; it could be to draw something specific into the wearer's life; or it could be a symbol to generate a certain kind of energy.

An *amulet* is used for protection. It can be something as simple as a stone charged with this intention, or a piece of paper inscribed with a pentagram.

A *talisman* is worn to attract a specific energy into the wearer's life: good fortune or peace. Again, this can be a stone, or a piece of jewellery charged or inscribed with a particular symbol.

A *charm* is worn or carried to attract a specific outcome. You might carry a love charm in your handbag, for example, and it could be a drawstring bag filled with various herbs and spices. Another charm could be a stone or crystal that you have charged and used in a spell.

Timing spells by the celestial bodies

Just as you have to pick the right type of spell to support your magical needs, you have to consider the timing of that spell. When is the best time to perform it and does this really affect the outcome? Yes, it does. You have to give your spell the best chance of working, and in order to do so you need to consider many factors. You are working with nature, with the energy that is all around you, so you need to connect to it. To do this you have to consider the Moon and its movements, the other planets, and how they move through the days of the week and the astrological signs.

Each day of the week is associated with a planet, and each planet has certain influences. To make your spell successful it needs to be carried out on the day that is best associated with your desire. That way, you are working with that planet's specific energies.

For most days, you can tell which planet rules which day from the names. Sunday is the Sun, Monday is the Moon, Tuesday is Mars, Wednesday is Mercury (the old rhyme says that Wednesday's child is full of woe: this doesn't refer to the feeling, but to the god Wodin who is linked to Mercury), Thursday is Jupiter, Friday is Venus, and Saturday is Saturn.

Below is a brief explanation of the magical significance of each planet including the metal associated with it. The metal can be used in spells as an offering to attract the specific energies you require.

The Sun

Ride too close and you will get burned, or so they say. The Sun is the great life-giver; its rays warm us, and nurture the Earth. So the Sun rules new life and is associated with warmth, glory, fame and success. It can also help with healing spells. The Sun is a masculine energy and can be used for strength in any area of life. The metal associated with the Sun is gold. Use this colour in any spells that require the Sun's specific energies.

The Moon

The mystical Moon casts her light over us, I say *her*, because the Moon is distinctly feminine. Her rays bathe us in soft moonlight. The Moon is very powerful and affects the tides. As humans our bodies are made up, in part, of water and in that respect the Moon also affects us, in particular our emotions. Many people experience 'Moon madness' around the time of the full Moon: they feel jittery, excited, and perhaps a little tense. The Moon is particularly useful in spells for women and in healing women's health problems. The Moon is also associated with creativity, and psychic abilities.

The goddess Hecate rules the Moon, and she is often called the Queen of the Witches because of her link to divination. She is the goddess to work with if you want to develop your psychic abilities. Hecate is represented as the maiden, the mother and the crone. These three aspects relate to the phases of the Moon, which are particularly important in magic. The maiden is the new Moon; the beginning of new life, and projects, the birth of something. This is a good time to work magic that involves a new enterprise. The mother is the full Moon (think of a pregnant woman with her swollen belly). The time of the full Moon is an auspicious and significant time when dreams can be realised and wish spells work particularly well. The crone represents the dark of the Moon, the time when the Moon wanes to darkness. Spells that break patterns and addictions are well suited to this time.

The Moon is associated with silver. Wear silver when you need to attract the Moon's attention. Moonstone can also be used in spells directly connected with the Moon's energies.

Jupiter

Jupiter is an interesting planet. It doesn't always give us what we expect. You can work with Jupiter when you want some assistance with career aspirations or money. However, Jupiter is said to give you more of what you already have, so, if you have very little money, then expect to receive the same.

Tin is the metal associated with this planet. If you are looking for success in business, inscribe your wishes into a piece of tin and carry it as a charm.

Mars

Mars is the god of war, so the planet represents power and aggression. It's a very masculine energy. Its energies can be used in a positive way. Work magic on a Tuesday when you need to be more assertive. Perhaps you have some kind of battle going on in your life and you need to assure a positive outcome, then ask Mars for help. Legal matters are also connected to Mars, as are justice and balance.

The metal linked to this planet is iron. Think about iron and its resistance to things, it cannot be bent easily, just as an assertive will cannot be affected by outside influences. Keep a piece of iron on you as a charm when you need strength in your life.

Mercury

Mercury is the god of communication, the winged messenger of the gods. Children born on a Wednesday are often very creative and gifted communicators. Work with Mercury when you need help in any area of communication or negotiation. You can also use this planet's energies to help with creative or business pursuits.

The metal associated with Mercury is... mercury!

Saturn

Saturn is linked to karma: what goes around comes around. This planet is associated with protection and breaking negative patterns. So, perform spells for cleansing, protection and to help you get rid of unwanted influences on a Saturday. Saturn can help you to overcome obstacles in any area of your life.

Lead is associated with this planet. Lead is heavy and absorbs negative vibes, so carry a piece in your pocket to help you to keep focused and to break bad habits.

Venus

Possibly the most well known of all the gods and goddesses, Venus is all about love. Work with her energies when you want to draw love and romance into your life. The planet is also associated with playfulness, sex, passion, fertility, healing and spells to help children.

The metal linked to Venus is copper. Place a piece of copper on your altar with some roses when you want to encourage Venus's loving energies to flow in your life.

Astrological associations

Each planet has a corresponding astrological sign and this is worth considering if you are working a spell for a particular sign. It is also useful to think about the parts of the body ruled by that particular sign. For instance, you might want a spell to help ease a sore throat and aid communication for an important meeting. In this case you might work with both Mercury (communication) and Venus, as Venus rules Taurus, the sign associated with the throat and neck.

The planets' astrological associations

Star sign	Ruling planet	Body parts governed
Aries	Mars	head
Taurus	Venus	neck, throat, shoulders
Gemini	Mercury	lungs, hands, arms
Cancer	Moon	breasts, stomach
Leo	Sun	heart, solar plexus
Virgo	Mercury	digestive system
Libra	Venus	kidneys, back
Scorpio	Mars	reproductive organs
Sagittarius	Saturn	thighs
Capricorn	Saturn	knees, bones
Aquarius	Uranus	calves, ankles, circulatory and glandular systems
Pisces	Jupiter	feet

The seasons

The seasons of the year play a very important role in our lives, even if we don't fully realise it. There are the obvious changes in temperature and weather that affect our daily routine, and though we may grumble about the wind and the rain or the ice on the roads, our environment needs these things to survive and flourish. In the witchy calendar, the seasons are marked and celebrated; each one is embraced for the particular gifts it brings.

Witchy festivals

There are special festivals and celebrations marked in every witch's calendar. These are times when a witch can give thanks and celebrate her chosen path, as well as a good excuse for a party! It's a good idea to mark these festivals with respect if you are dabbling in the magical arts, and find your own way of celebrating them. You can even perform spells at this time that relate to the festival.

Samhain or Halloween

Perhaps the most famous festival widely associated with witchcraft is Halloween. Today Halloween is highly commercialised and seen as a bit of fun, a time when children can dress up in scary costumes and go out trick or treating. This commercialisation comes from the USA, but there is much more to the festival than first meets the eye if we delve into its history.

Halloween gets its name from All Hallows' Eve, a Roman Catholic festival, and the Catholics in turn took the festival from the pagans who called it (and still do) Samhain, pronounced *Sow-wain*. This is a very special time for witches. It's a time when the veil between life and death is thin, and spirits are said to wander – hence the spooky connotations. Witches, however, don't see this as particularly scary; it's meant to be a time to honour the dead, to remember and cherish them. The pagans would burn fires on Halloween night to light a path for the dead and show them the way home. They would also lay a place at the table for their dearly departed as a mark of respect.

Halloween also marks the coming of winter. It's a time of withdrawal and hibernation, when the Earth replenishes itself ready for spring. As such it's a time to let go of things; a time to break ties and bad habits and also to re-evaluate your life and look at your accomplishments.

If you would like to mark this festival, consider carrying out a small ceremony for your lost loved ones. It doesn't have to be anything elaborate. Lighting a candle and saying a prayer is enough to show respect. You may wish to lay an extra place at your table, to welcome the spirit of your departed just as the pagans did all those years ago. Halloween is also a good time to perform spells that release you from things, so, if you'd like to break a bad habit or get rid of unwanted influences in your life, try the following ritual.

Halloween ritual

Take a piece of paper and write down what you want to eliminate from your life. Next light a white candle. Concentrate on your breathing and, as with other visualisations, imagine that you are breathing in light and love and breathing out any negative and unwanted feelings.

When you have done this for a few minutes, take the paper and burn it in the flame of the candle. Gather the ash together, and take it outside to your garden. If you don't have a garden, take it to your local park, or use a window basket.

Bury the ash deep in the ground or soil. As you do so, say the following:

I am released from all my woes,

on Samhain Eve the blessing goes,

to take away the ties that bind,

and free me, body, soul and mind.

So mote it be!

Other important witchy festivals

Imbolc

This is sometimes referred to as the Festival of Lights. It's held on 2 February and marks the beginning of the year and new growth. It's an ancient fertility festival. *Imbolc* is an old Celtic meaning *in the belly*. This is an excellent time to focus on new projects and to carry out spells that stimulate and promote new ideas and enterprises, as well as fertility spells. Use green and white candles in magic at this time.

Beltane

Beltane is the Wicca fertility festival held on 30 April. It's also known as May Eve. It's a time to celebrate and nurture the land and give thanks to the Earth goddess. As it's a fertility festival, it would be the ideal time for those trying to get pregnant to perform a ritual or spell. You can mark this time of year by decorating your altar with plenty of fresh flowers. Burn brown, green or pink candles and offer up your thanks to Mother Earth for everything she provides. You can also bake cakes and bread as part of the magical rite for growth and stability. Remember to visualise your aims while baking and eating!

Lammas

Lammas or 'loaf-mass' is celebrated on 1 August, and marks the beginning of autumn. In particular, it celebrates the waning of the Sun god, and the abundance of the Earth. This is a good time to give thanks for all the blessings in your life. To celebrate Lammas, light a candle and give thanks for the radiant and life-giving beauty of the Sun. This is also a good time to perform magic to help bring your dreams and aims to fruition. Burn gold, yellow or orange candles in your spells and celebrations to honour the Sun.

CHAPTER FOUR

A house witch's store cupboard

Some rules and thoughts on spell-casting ★★

As with any craft, there are always rules and regulations to consider before you begin. These are not restrictive. If anything, we adhere to rules because they help us to get the best out of something, and they prevent us from harming ourselves or others.

Witchcraft is not evil. The act of magic is not evil. It is only evil if the person behind the act harbours negative intentions. In this case, the energy associated with the spell becomes dark and for an entirely different purpose. Magic is like anything in life: if you enter into it with positive, loving thoughts, it's going to be a positive experience for you and anyone else involved; but if you are negative and hateful, you will make it a negative experience all round.

Many witches follow what is called the Wiccan Rede. This states, 'An it harm none, do what thou wilt.' In other words, as long as your magic harms no one, go ahead and do it. Of course this calls into question what we mean by 'harm'. We are not necessarily talking about physical harm here; there are many ways and levels that you can affect people.

As mentioned earlier, magic is a positive force, and it should never be used to manipulate or control a person. It should never be used to force events upon another person. Some witches refuse to perform spells on people unless they have their agreement beforehand. This is not always possible. In the case of a very sick relative who desperately needs a healing spell, you might not be able to obtain this agreement, but because the spell is for the all-round good, it would be safe to go ahead with it.

Some witches also believe in the Law of Threefold Return. This is the belief that anything you do is returned to you three times over. So, if you carry out good deeds then they will be magnified back to you; but if you use your magic for darker purposes, you will receive negative energies times three. This might sound frightening, but it's actually a good benchmark for magical work. Take each spell individually and think about your intentions, then ask yourself if you would like this reflected back upon you. If the answer is yes, then you know that you are coming from a good place. If the answer is no, or you aren't sure, perhaps you should rethink your purpose.

Witchcraft is about making the world a better place. It's about taking responsibility for your life, and changing what you can by tapping into your individual power. Use magic in a responsible way and it will work wonders; use it flippantly and with no respect and the results will be disappointing, and can backfire.

Using everyday ingredients in magic

Your witch's store cupboard is at your fingertips. You don't have to go in search of special and obscure ingredients; you probably have everything you need in your kitchen right now. Common herbs, spices and other foods all have magical properties and can be used in spells.

The simple act of cooking is a spell. Deciding on the ingredients, on the flavour you want, and the ambience, is magical. If you've ever prepared a special meal for the one you love, you will have performed a spell without realising it. You have planned a romantic evening, your aim being to inspire and encourage love. You have chosen each course with this in mind, and lovingly prepared it in the hope that it adds to the atmosphere. You have used magic. The same goes for dinner parties, or meals planned to entertain guests and work colleagues. Your intentions may be different – you want to impress your boss, promote feelings of friendship and cooperation – but you have used food and cooking methods in a spell to achieve your aims.

So, as it's that easy, what do you have lurking in your cupboards and how can it be of use? In the next few pages you will find various items and the types of spells they can be used in. This is only a brief selection – a taster to get you started.

Herbs and spices

Herbs, spices, plants and flowers have been used in magic for centuries. Each one has particular properties and a magical vibration and is used in different ways. You can brew them as potions or teas; burn them along with oils to scent a room or put them in pouches to make charms which can be carried about your person to draw love, good fortune and protection. The simple act of giving flowers is magical; it can make someone feel a million dollars! Here are some witchy essentials you might already have. If not, they are all inexpensive and easy to get hold of or grow in your garden.

Basil

Basil is the money herb. The large, fat leaves are likened to notes.

Grow pots of basil about the house to encourage the flow of money. Steep basil leaves in hot water then drain the liquid into your floor wash to encourage prosperity. Sprinkle basil leaves in your bath and, as you immerse yourself, visualise a fountain of money washing over you, see yourself surrounded by money and know that you are well looked after. Basil can also be used with rose petals in love spells. It promotes feelings of abundance.

Bay

Bay leaves aid psychic development. Burn them to increase your psychic powers and to encourage prophetic dreams. Take a dried leaf and write a wish on it, then burn it in the flame of a candle on the night of a full Moon.

Cardamom

Again, another useful herb for love and romance; the white pods are particularly good for matters of the heart; the green for business success. Cardamom adds oomph and sparkle to any love mixtures.

Cinnamon

Cinnamon is a wonderful warming spice which draws success and good fortune. If you require speedy success, and you're taking a test of any sort, carry a piece of cinnamon in your pocket. Burn the oil, and use the spice in charm bags for success.

Note: Cinnamon oil against skin can cause irritation!

Cloves

Carry a clove in a charm bag to attract the opposite sex. Burned cloves also attract money. Use cloves in any spell where you need extra pulling power.

Coriander

Coriander is used in spells to promote love and lust. You can burn the seeds or leaves, or sprinkle them over food and eat them while picturing a loving environment. You can also use coriander in a love charm and carry it about your person with a handful of cloves to attract a mate.

Cumin

This spice promotes happiness. It can also be used to ward off evil influences. Sprinkle it about your house to keep away those that wish you harm.

Dill

Dill is often used in love magic. It can stimulate enthusiasm and exhilaration, and is often used to pep up a failing love life. Dill is a must for any romantic meals and wishes.

Ginger

Ginger is used in love spells. If you want to bless a relationship and keep the love burning strong, take two ginger roots of a similar size, bind them together with red ribbon and keep them in a safe place. Perform this spell on a Friday (the day ruled by Venus) and say a few simple words to promote your love. Eating ginger brings energy and fast luck. Ginger adds fire and a speedy response to any spell.

Mint

Mint is used in healing and love potions. It's particularly good for digestion. Fresh mint leaves can be rubbed on the forehead to ease a headache. Mint is a protective herb. Many witches lay mint leaves on their altar to draw good spirits. Burn peppermint and rose oil to promote love; you could also add mint to any dish when you want to inspire love.

Nutmeg

Often referred to as the gambler's charm, nutmeg brings good luck in any situation. Rub the oil into your palms before you play cards and you will have a lucky streak. Burn the oil and let the fresh aroma draw good fortune. Sprinkle nutmeg over food while visualising success.

Parsley

Parsley has been used for years in magical preparations to ward off evil. A sprig of parsley on your plate will lift the vibrations and protect you. Eat parsley to increase your strength and ardour. You can also use it in magical baths for this purpose, and to draw money quickly.

Rosemary

Often referred to as the women's herb; wherever you find rosemary growing, you will find a strong and powerful woman. Rosemary can be used to add extra bite to your spells. It's a cleansing herb that promotes positive vibrations about the house. If you need a pick me up, steep some rosemary in hot water, drain the liquid, add a spoonful of honey and fresh mint, and drink. Rosemary is good for mental alertness and clarity – it's a great herb to use before a test.

Sage

As well as being excellent in cooking, sage purifies and cleanses. Burn a handful of the leaves, then let the smoke waft about your house to get rid of negative energies. Sage also soothes sore throats and can be used in teas for this purpose. If you don't like the taste, either add honey to sweeten, or use it to gargle with or as a mouth rinse.

Thyme

Thyme purifies a space of negative energy. Burn it with sage before performing any spells to cleanse your casting circle. Carried in a charm bag, thyme brings good health. Some believe that if you place a sprig of thyme beneath your pillow you will have a restful sleep. To make a sleep pillow, fill a small cushion or pouch with thyme and lavender, sew it up and place it beneath your usual pillow.

Vervain

This herb can be used in spells for love, money and protection. Carry any part of the plant as an amulet or in a charm pouch. If vervain grows in the garden or house it will attract money and prosperity. It's been claimed that the juice from the plant can cure almost anything, but watch out: drinking it may make you lose your sexual appetite!

Other food items

Apples

Apples have been used in magic for centuries. Cut an apple in half vertically and you will see the sacred symbol of the pentagram often worn by witches. Apples are particularly potent in love spells. Leave an apple under a tree on a Friday as a gift for Venus and ask that she bless you with true love. Bake an apple pie with a special wish for love, then serve it to your partner. Carve both of your initials in the pastry.

Bananas

A wonderful fruit for male fertility and virility, a banana can be eaten or the skin can be rubbed on the body to increase stamina and sexual appetite.

Bread

The act of making bread is very magical and works wonderfully in spells to boost your financial situation. If you're looking for a promotion at work, bake a loaf of bread on a Wednesday and visualise an increase in money. Ask Mercury to help you find the right words to secure that promotion and improve your finances. You don't have to bake the loaf from scratch: using a bread maker is just as effective as long as you keep the visualisation going and have clear intentions.

Coffee

The aroma of freshly made coffee is said to aid concentration and increase efficiency in the workplace. You don't have to drink the coffee; simply smelling the beans is enough to provide a burst of mental alertness. Sharing coffee in a work environment promotes cooperation and communication. What better excuse is there for more coffee breaks?

Eggs

Eggs have countless magical uses. They are wonderful in ridding a person of negative energies or influences. If someone has harmful powers over you, write their name on an egg and place the egg in the freezer. This freezes the person's abilities to control or manipulate you. If you have an unpleasant habit that you'd like to get rid of, write it on the shell of an egg, place the egg on newspaper at your feet and stamp on it while saying: *'Be gone from my life, I am no longer tied. From this moment on I am free to decide. Be gone from my life, be gone far away. This is a new start, it is as I say!'* Remove the broken egg and newspaper from your house. Eggs in their shells can be rubbed gently over the body to heal and draw out badness. Eggs can also be eaten to strengthen fertility.

Honey

Honey is associated with Oshun, a goddess of love and beauty. Honey is a lovely ingredient that can be used in love, fertility and money spells. Bathe in warm water, honey and rose petals to encourage love and inspire beauty. Add honey to magical teas to help soothe and increase self esteem. Take a spoonful of honey and pumpkin seeds if you want to improve your fertility, and visualise a strong healthy womb as you do so. Honey is also known for its antibacterial properties, so it can be used in teas for healing and also on wounds. Manuka is the best type of honey for this.

Lemons

Lemon juice works particularly well in love magic. Burn lemon oil with rose to draw love and romance. Add a couple of drops of lemon juice to any tea to cleanse and purify.

Lettuce

Lettuce promotes feelings of peace and harmony. Make an infusion of lettuce tea to drink before you go to bed, as it helps to induce calm and sleep and encourage peaceful dreams.

Milk

Milk has wonderful nurturing and healing properties. It can also be used in protection spells. Bathe in milk on a Monday when the Moon is full and ask for her beautiful rays to protect you and increase your personal power. Milk is often used in spells for beauty and youth.

Nuts

Nuts are gifts from the trees and as such are considered sacred and very magical. All nuts assist with fertility and wealth, but some have other attributes too. Hazelnuts, for example, are considered to imbue you with wisdom. Chestnuts promote love. Pine nuts encourage good health, vitality and also love. The key when eating any nut is visualisation. Double nuts are considered to be incredibly lucky and make excellent charms for good fortune.

Onions

Onions ward off evil vibrations and cleanse a space. Chop an onion and place it around the house to keep out unwanted visitors and absorb negative energy.

Oranges

Oranges are associated with love magic. Orange oil can be burned and used to anoint pink candles when you want to attract love. Use orange oil with red candles when you want to spice up your love life. Eating a fresh fruit salad of oranges, strawberries and raspberries increases self-esteem, and when shared with a partner helps to promote romance and playfulness.

Potatoes

Carry potatoes to alleviate aches and pains. They are also good in spells to aid slimming. Carve your name into the potato, then, as you peel it, imagine the weight falling away (see full details of this spell in Chapter 10: Spells for health and well-being). See yourself at your desired shape and size. Eat potatoes when you need grounding and comfort.

Rice

Rice is used in prosperity and money spells. Whenever you cook rice, visualise money coming into your pocket and growing, just as the rice swells and grows in the pot. Fill a jar with rice and bury it in your garden, preferably on a full or new Moon in early spring. Imagine it is a pot of gold. Ask that as the garden grows and flourishes so does your financial situation. When your financial situation improves, dig up your pot of gold and thank Mother Nature for providing you with everything you need.

Seeds

Like nuts, seeds can be used in money and fertility magic. Pumpkin seeds work particularly well in fertility spells. Eat them, or sprinkle them around a green candle while visualising new growth. Sesame seeds are good for increasing finances.

Sugar

Sugar can be used to draw love. It has powerful properties of attraction. Sprinkle sugar on a pink candle, light it and visualise the type of partner you want to attract.

Wine

While it is not recommended to drink wine during spells, you can seal your magic at the end with a glass of wine as a thank-you to the Goddess. Red wine works best for love magic, and white wine for protection and healing spells. Celebrate the success of your spell by saluting the powers of the Earth and thanking your Inner Goddess for her power and guidance.

Flowers and plants

Daffodil

These lovely yellow flowers are wonderful pick-me-ups. Use them to cure depression and invite friendly spirits into your home. Give bunches to your friends to heal any rifts and strengthen the bonds between you.

Dandelion

Dandelions increase psychic potential. Make a tea from the flowers and drink it on a full Moon to encourage prophetic dreams. Drink the tea daily to exercise those psychic muscles.

Geranium

Pink and red geranium flowers are used in love spells. The essential oil is burned to help heal and balance emotions. A vase of geraniums placed in the home will protect it.

Honeysuckle

If honeysuckle grows outside your house, you will be blessed with good luck. Place flowers in a vase in your home to attract money and good fortune. The flowers can be crushed and used in potions which, when rubbed on the forehead, increase psychic powers.

Lavender

Lavender smells lovely and has uplifting properties. Use it in sachets or spell pouches to enhance happiness and well-being. Burn lavender oil to increase positive energy in your home, or place a dab on your temples the next time you have a headache. Lavender is relaxing and can be sewn into pillows for sleep.

Nettle

Nettles purify and cleanse. Drink the tea to rid your body of toxins and strengthen your spirit. An infusion of nettle leaves can be used as a final rinse when washing hair to promote its growth and vitality.

Rose

Rose is the flower of love and romance. Fresh or dried rose petals can be used in charm bags to attract love. Use with cloves to increase attraction and turn heads. Sprinkle rose petals in the bath when you want some romantic attention. Red and pink roses promote love, Yellow and orange ones inspire and seal the bonds of friendship. Keep vases of fresh roses about the house to encourage the flow of love.

Mixing and matching

The key to successful magic is to make it personal. I have suggested guidelines on types of ingredients and their possible uses; now it's up to you. Play, experiment, try different combinations, but most importantly do what feels right. You might feel that a certain food that isn't mentioned here has a special property and can be used in a spell – go for it; trust your instincts to try it. Investigate! There's a wealth of reading material on magical ingredients. The items I have mentioned are only the tip of the iceberg. Have fun uncovering the magical attributes of other everyday ingredients.

You can put things together in a variety of ways. Say a few words, make up a chant or a rhyme, or say nothing at all. It's entirely up to you. One point to reinforce: if you do choose to say a few words, always keep it in the present. Say it like you already have it! For example, if you wanted some good luck or a change of fortune, it would be better to say, 'I am lucky. Lady Fortune is with me. I am blessed,' rather than, 'I draw good luck to me, my fortune is changing for the better, I will be blessed.' The last phrase puts what you want in the future, and that's where it will stay. If you say it in the present, then you will receive it in the present.

Magical tools

To perform magic, you don't need an array of special tools. The magic comes from you, and that's the most important thing to remember. As with any craft, though, tools can and do help. This doesn't mean that you have to go out and buy expensive accessories, unless you want to. Most magical tools are readily available at home. You'll be amazed at the variety of everyday objects which can be used for witchcraft.

Once you start using these objects for spells, it would be wise to keep them specifically for that purpose. In other words, if you take a pot from your kitchen for boiling herbal infusions and potions, keep it separate from your usual cooking utensils. For it to assist in your magical work, it has to be given purpose and treated with respect. This cannot happen if it is used for all manner of things.

So what does the modern witch need to help her with spell casting? Here are some of the essentials that you may well already have in your home.

Pestle and mortar

The trusty pestle and mortar is an absolute essential for modern mistresses of magic. Its use is obvious: to grind up herbs and spices for spells, lotions and potions. Be sure to spend the time while you are grinding wisely, and visualise, visualise, visualise!

Cauldron (pot)

I say *cauldron*, but I'm not suggesting you should go out and buy a traditional one unless you really want to. A dedicated cooking pot works just as well, as long as it's something you can boil liquids in for your spells.

Wand

A wand is used to direct magical energy. You might want to use it to charge an amulet or stone by pointing at the object while visualising your aims and speaking a spell. A wand can be made from anything. Some witches prefer special woods (willow, rowan and birch are particular favourites), but a length of twig from your garden will work just as well. I have even heard that some witches on the move use umbrellas as a way of directing magical energy; if you have a surplus of umbrellas, that's fine, although you might get some strange looks if you start pointing or waving them about in public! Liquorice sticks also make excellent wands.

Mirror

The magical mirror is another simple item essential for any witchy woman. It's something that's easy to carry about your person, and can be used for magic on the move. A make-up compact is perfect, or a hand-held mirror – the choice is yours. Remember to keep this mirror just for your magical spells.

To charge and cleanse it, leave it out over night during a full Moon. You can also charge it with the powerful rays of the Sun by holding it in sunlight for a few seconds. You don't need long, and be careful not to reflect the burning rays onto anyone else, or anything that might catch fire! As you hold the mirror, say a few words such as, *I charge you with the glory of the Sun, be filled with light. So mote it be.*

Broom

I wouldn't suggest you try to fly one, but brooms are very handy magical tools for cleansing an area of negative vibes. All you have to do is sweep the area and visualise it being cleansed by the brushing actions. The broom represents both male and female energies, the broom handle being the male aspect, and the straw head being female.

Book of shadows

This is not some scary ancient text, although there are many old 'grimoires' that contain spells used hundreds of years ago. Your book of shadows is your record of the spells that you perform. It's just like a recipe book. You write down the spell, the ingredients you used and any other details that you think might be useful. It's also the place to record your successes, thoughts and feelings. You might also like to use this book as a journal in which to note down your visualisations or dreams.

This book is for you, so organise it in any way you choose. It is your record, something for you to refer back to and delve into when the need arises. Some witches even keep their book of shadows on disk. Again, this is down to personal choice, but you might find it suits you to type your thoughts directly into the computer.

Spell boxes

Boxes come in all shapes and sizes and most (though not cardboard ones so much) can be useful when it comes to magic. They can store magical tools, herbs and spices. They can also be used as a spell box, which means that the box is intrinsically part of the spell. You would fill the box with items to support the magic, you might even choose to carve or draw a picture on the box that is linked with your magical aim, and then place it on your altar.

Enchanting associates

Inventing your magical self

The kind of magical workings talked about so far in this book can be performed on your own. You are solely responsible for them and you don't need the help of others to achieve your aims. You certainly don't need to be part of a coven or group to carry out *any* of the spells in this book. However, as with many things in life, it helps to have friends in high places, and a few powerful tips on hand!

Most of us have a network of trusty friends to call upon when we need some guidance or support, not to mention a few feminine wiles and tricks of the trade to help get us through trying times! Magic can be helped along in the same way.

When we perform a spell, we have to believe in it and our own power to make it work, therefore magic requires a good dose of self-belief. Magic is about accessing the powers that exist inside us and in our surroundings. To do this, we develop a magical persona, we are the witch. We have that power. Whether we picture ourselves as one of the sassy charmed ones, or more of a superhero diva, it doesn't matter. We have an image; we have an inner strength that we tap into.

Now this is the fun bit! We can create that persona to include anything we want and call upon it at any time during our daily routine. Think about it for a second: say you're having trouble in a meeting at work – perhaps you're dealing with a difficult client – all it takes is a quiet moment of visualisation, a simple spell in the head and you can don your magical persona and create miracles. It really is as simple as that.

The key to creating this alter ego and making the power work for you is in giving yourself a magical name. It may sound like child's play, but many witches use magical names in their spell work. It's a way of raising power, of tuning into that part of themselves where the will resides. The magical name you give yourself is private and personal to you. You do not have to reveal it to anyone. You may choose to, particularly if you do become part of a coven and carry out rituals together, but you have complete control, so it is your decision.

Choosing a magical name

Goddesses

Choosing a magical name might seem as simple as picking your favourite name out of thin air. In actual fact, finding the right magical name can be a lengthy and discerning task. Some witches choose to name themselves after a particular goddess that they admire. This can be useful, particularly if you want to take on some of the qualities of this goddess, or use some of her magical skills in your spells. I suggest investing in a good book about goddesses and reading as much as you can on each one, to be sure you choose the right one for you.

You will find that there are many different variations when it comes to goddesses and names, depending on the culture and country. For example Venus is the Roman goddess of love, but she is based on Aphrodite, essentially the same goddess of love, but the Ancient Greek version. Mythologies from around the world often blend together, and you will find similarities in each one.

Totem animals

A totem is an entity, often an animal spirit, that watches over you. So, another popular choice for magical names is to find your totem or power animal and incorporate this into your name. This is something Native Americans do as part of their spirituality. They revere animals and have a great respect for them. They believe that when you work with a creature's specific attributes, you are working with their medicine.

To discover your power animal consider the following. Are you drawn to any particular animal or bird? What characteristics does this species have that you admire and want to draw into your life? Do a little research into this. If you feel drawn to a particular creature, find out as much about its nature, behaviour and cultural associations as you can. This will help you to establish why you are drawn to it, what need it fulfils in you.

Power animals are often changeable depending on what is going on in your life, and the type of magic that you want to work. So as you progress through different periods in your life, you will have different totem animals to help you on your journey.

You might need an extra dose of courage and fire for a particular task, for example, so you might draw upon the lion to help you through this period. You might want to do some visualisation work with lions to help build up your confidence and bravery. At another time in your life, you might need assistance in psychic development and broadening your knowledge, therefore you might feel drawn to the owl. Again, look into the mythology and natural history of the creature you have chosen to see if it fits with how you think and feel.

As you look into this more you will also find that each goddess has particular totem creatures associated with her. So, depending on your affinity with the goddess you might choose to incorporate one of these in your magical name. Use the images of your power animal in your magical work, include them in visualisations and find out what message they have for you.

Here are few popular totem animals and their associations.

Bear

Bears represent wisdom. Bears spend part of the year in hibernation. They retreat to their caves and withdraw from life in order to replenish themselves. Therefore, they represent spending time in solace, and retreating into our spiritual selves in the effort of transformation and rejuvenation. Bears are also linked with healing, and in Native American traditions, the healer of the tribe would often use bear medicine and wear bear skins while performing healing rituals. Bears use the secrets of herbs. They are strong and powerful and, contrary to popular belief, only tend to attack if they are cornered.

Call on bear medicine when: you need to reflect upon a situation or you need a deeper insight into an area of your life. Also use bear medicine to help with healing and working with herbs.

Hawk

Hawks are extremely powerful birds, able to soar high in the sky and spot prey from a remarkable distance. Their gaze is clear and far-reaching and they do not miss a trick! Hawk medicine helps you to see beyond the surface of things. It keeps you mentally alert and agile, able to perceive things on many levels.

Draw on hawk medicine when: you need clarity, or when you feel that you don't know all the facts about a situation. The hawk will help you see beyond the physical.

Dog

Man's best friend, dogs are known for their infinite loyalty, their warmth and their trusting natures. They are also patient and steadfast. If you want to nurture these qualities in yourself, call upon dog medicine to open your heart and help you trust in yourself and others. Dogs are honest and consistent.

Use the power of the dog when: you need to stick to a goal and remain open-hearted.

Bee

This may be an unlikely choice for a totem animal, but bees are incredibly industrious creatures. They are nature's alchemists. They work hard and as a team. They create through sheer hard work, determination and cooperation.

Call upon bee medicine when: you need to apply yourself to a task, when you need to be more industrious and focused. You can also use bee medicine when you need to work in a team and foster a spirit of helpful communication.

Horse

Native Americans have a deep admiration and respect for horses. The horse was the creature that carried them from one place to another; it was an extension of their being. The horse was hard-working and strong. It travelled at speed, and could keep going for long distances.

Look to the horse for assistance when: you need strength and stamina. Its graceful power will support you and carry you forward.

Wolf

Wolves are beautiful animals. They are excellent hunters, agile and clever; they work as a team to capture their prey. They are also one of the few creatures that mate for life.

Use wolf medicine when: you need to boost your mental abilities, and in particular when you have a specific aim or target. The wolf will help you to think on your feet; will keep you primed and flexible.

Rabbit

You may wonder how rabbits can be of assistance; after all, they're pretty good at mating, but what else can they do? Well, in fact, rabbits work on instinct; they are tuned into fear, and act upon it, darting away when they sense danger. This ability to feel fear and work with it is part of rabbit medicine. Fear is a good thing, and a necessary part of life.

Tap into rabbit medicine when: you need to face your fears. The rabbit will help you to use your fear productively.

Fox

Cunning and devious are words that are often used to describe foxes. They are resourceful and clever. They scavenge for survival, many living in the urban jungle and making a success out of most situations. There is much we can learn from these intelligent creatures. They are creative and make best use of their surroundings.

Call upon fox medicine when: you need to be resourceful, when you need to turn something into a success. The fox will help you to transform a problem into an opportunity.

Owl

Owls are fascinating birds. They are nocturnal, their piercing gaze cutting through the darkness. They have long been associated with wisdom and knowledge, and in folklore they are often linked with death and the occult. Owl medicine is about developing your sixth sense, seeing through the veil and beyond. It's about psychic potential and growth, and the magical arts. Owls are often associated with the goddess Hecate, the Queen of the Witches.

Use owl medicine to: help you tune into your intuition and trust your instincts.

Trees, plants and flowers

Just as animals and mythical creatures can feature in your name and assist you in magical work, so can trees, plants and flowers. This makes perfect sense, because witchcraft is based in and around nature. Witches draw upon the infinite power of Mother Nature. They use certain plants and flowers in spells. They celebrate the Earth and nurture it. They understand the ebb and flow of the seasons, of the Moon and the planets. Again it is worth spending some time researching these things. Every plant and flower has an association with a planet, and has a range of qualities and uses. Look into each one and decide which might help you in your life and therefore be most appropriate in your magical persona.

Visualisation

Native Americans are known for their Vision Quests. Such a quest often involved a young brave spending time (sometimes days and nights) on his own, without food or water, in deep meditation to discover his true purpose in life. This was a difficult ordeal, but the challenge and hardship were part of the quest and the results were life changing.

I'm not suggesting you deprive yourself of your morning latté (although cutting out caffeine does assist psychic development and creativity), and I certainly don't advocate going without sustenance, but it is worth spending some time in reflection when searching for your magical name. The more time you spend internally reflecting upon your aims and objectives, the more focused your power will be, the clearer your mind, and the happier you will be as a person, because knowing yourself brings peace and balance. It is highly beneficial to have some quiet time in the midst of the chaos of a busy life.

Try this visualisation to help you find your magical name. You can also adapt this to discover your totem animal.

Find your magical name

Sit cross-legged on the floor, your shoulders relaxed, your eyes closed. Begin by focusing on your breathing. With every breath you take in, imagine that a stream of light is entering your body. This light is filled with energy and warmth. With every breath you exhale, imagine that you are ridding your body of toxins, of negativity, fear and pain. Continue to do this until you feel relaxed and your mind is quietened from the usual internal chatter. Now you are ready to begin.

In your mind's eye, see a door – a golden elaborate door. This door will lead you into another world – the world of your subconscious. When you are ready, open the door and step inside. What do you see? If you find it hard to immerse yourself in this world, imagine that the door opens up into the beautiful lush green countryside, with the sun shining and a forest in the distance. Where you find yourself doesn't matter. This is your world, your picture and you can go anywhere you like.

Try to take in all the details. What does this place smell like? How do you feel standing here? Can you hear any sounds? Can you see any movement? What is the weather like? Take a deep breath and begin to explore. You can walk as far as you like. You can stop when you want to.

When you are ready, take a moment and sit. What are you sitting on? How does it feel? In the distance you see movement; something or someone is coming towards you. Wait for a minute as the figure gets closer. Who is it?

Remember this is your world and you are in control: you can turn and open the door and return to your conscious mind at any time.

The visitor has a message for you. They are here to help you find your magical name. Ask them what it is. What do they have to tell you? Perhaps they cannot speak and prefer to draw letters in the earth. Perhaps they give you a gift or leave you with a feeling. Let the story unfold as it feels right to you.

When you are ready, thank the magical stranger for their gift and begin to journey back to the door and step through into your conscious mind. Take a few moments to focus on your breathing before opening your eyes.

Now write about the experience in your magical journal. What did you see? What did you learn about yourself? Note down the impressions you had. It doesn't matter if you don't find your magical name the first time you try this visualisation. It could take several attempts. The most important thing is that you enjoy the experience and learn something about yourself in the process.

Magical names can come to you in a number of ways. Sometimes you need to search for them for quite a while, and in some cases someone might give you a name just like that, and it feels right. Perhaps somebody inadvertently gifts you with the name. The most important thing to remember is that the name is right for you. Once you have your name, you can use it in magical work, inscribe it in candles or chant it to summon your individual power. Write it on charms and amulets. You can use it in so many different types of spells to remind you of the strength and magic that live within.

Making friends in high places

We've all heard the phrase 'friends in high places', but it couldn't be more apt for us magically inclined women! You only have to know where to look and how to connect with the right helpers, and you have a wealth of friends who can support you in your aims. Let's consider a few, and how you can enlist their help.

Spirit guides

Everyone has a spirit guide. Some people have more than one. They are out there in the spirit world watching over us, helping when they can – the unseen hand that pulls you back from the kerb as a car goes speeding past, the little voice in your head that says, 'Don't trust that man.' Any number of synchronicities in life can be down to our spirit guides as they try to communicate with us.

Spirit guides have our best interests at heart. They may be relatives that have passed over and keep a watchful eye on us; they may be complete strangers from another time in this world. They are linked to us, and endeavour to communicate with us through thoughts, feelings and dreams. The more you develop your psychic skills through visualisation and magical work, the more you will become aware of your spirit guide.

One of the easiest ways to employ the help of your guide and to instigate a relationship is through dreams. Take a piece of amethyst and place it beneath your pillow. (Amethyst is a wonderful crystal for opening up psychic channels of communication.) Just before you go to sleep, ask your spirit guide to enter your dreams. If you have a particular problem ask them for guidance. Spirit guides love to be of service! Make a note of what you dream that night, even if it doesn't make any sense at the time. Then, over the next few nights, repeat the practice. When you look back at your dreams, certain symbols or images might jump out at you; there might be recurring themes. These are signs that your spirit guide is trying to make a connection with you.

Angels

It's a nice thought that we might all have a guardian angel, and here's the great news – it's true! The angels are out there watching over us. There is a wealth of evidence when it comes to angel sightings and communication, and you only have to do a little digging to discover the truth behind this belief. There are angels for everything, from giving birth to finding a car park space. There are angels of justice and angels who protect and care for you.

You can ask the angels for help at any time in your life. A simple wish or prayer is enough to capture the attention of your angel. You could try guided visualisations if you want to encounter your personal guardian angel, or you might simply light a candle to your angel and give thanks for all the unseen wonders that they bring to your life.

Fairies

It might be a long time since you believed in fairies at the bottom of your garden, and it might seem childish, but many witches are convinced of their existence. There is an abundance of fairy folklore from all the corners of the globe, and the tales are magical to read.

There are those who believe that fairies were actually a nomadic tribe who wandered from place to place, stealing babies and generally causing all sorts of magical mayhem. Others believe they are flower spirits – tiny magical beings that are drawn to specific flowers and herbs. Much of the folklore states that fairies would enter into deals with humans and on more than one occasion trick them. Some tales suggest that fairies were helpful creatures that could be (and still are) invoked to assist with magical work.

There are common elements to attracting fairy magic into your world. Fairies love flowers and herbs, so be sure to have plenty of wild flowers growing in your garden. In particular, they love foxgloves, forget-me-nots, honeysuckle, primrose and lavender. They are also attracted by herbs, and their particular favourites are said to be thyme and rosemary. Some witches decorate their gardens with wind chimes and crystals to attract fairies, as they love music and pretty things. Whether these work or not, they definitely make for a pleasant natural environment and a talking point at barbecues!

Elementals

Elementals rule the elements. Each time you work with a particular element in magic, you are calling upon the elementals associated with it. There are four key elements that you can invoke to help you with your magic: earth, air, fire and water.

Each element is associated with particular spirits and with a direction and a colour, and if you want to work with elementals, you could incorporate these into your spells.

Element	Direction	Colour	Spirit
Air	East	Yellow	Sylphs
Fire	South	Red	Salamanders
Water	West	Blue	Undines (water spirits) and mermaids
Earth	North	Green	Gnomes and goblins

Some people believe that if you stare into the flames of a fire long enough you will see the fire elementals dancing. I would not advise doing this, as you are more likely to scorch your eyeballs!

The pentagram, a universal symbol worn for protection by witches, represents the elements (the fifth point of the star which is at the top relates to the spirit). The inverted pentagram (with two points at the top) which is often associated with evil, actually relates to the second degree initiation. This is something that happens in covens when witches go through a series of initiation rites.

There are many more spirits and entities out there that can assist in spells and magic. It's true that some of the traditional tales could (and should) be taken with a pinch of salt, but it's well worth looking into the folklore behind these stories as there are strong elements of truth lurking there

Part Two
Spells

Part 2 of the book is dedicated to spells.
I have organised the spells into chapters
covering love, success, money, work, home,
health, and a variety of other matters. The
spells are easy to perform, and most of them
use ingredients that you are likely to have
already at home. Each chapter begins with a
brief explanation of the type of spell and a
list of useful ingredients. You are encouraged
to experiment with these, and make up
your own spells or adapt the ones
I have suggested.
Let the magic begin!

CHAPTER SIX

Spells for love, relationships and sex

Love makes the world go round. All you need is love. Can't help falling in love... and so it goes on. There are thousands of songs and poems and proverbs that try to capture the essence of love. Let's face it, it's a universal emotion and essential to who we are. We all need love, we all give love and, if we're lucky, our lives are filled with the stuff. And yet this one glorious feeling can cause us so much pain too – the seeking of it, the holding on to it and of course the losing it, whether through a silly mistake or no fault of our own. Fate has much to do with the circumstances of this emotion. Love is a very important thing to us as humans, and as women. Some claim that women are governed more by the heart than men, but I think rather that women tend to be less scared by the power of emotions.

As women and witches, we use the power of this emotion in our magic. We focus our actions with love, so that every magical spell is empowered and carried out with the very best of intentions. So, love is imperative to us, as is being able to love freely and without fear.

Love spells can be potent, particularly if they are carried out in the right environment and at the right time. They can have wonderful results. A note of caution to stress, however: *Love spells should never be used to control or manipulate another's feelings.* You cannot make someone love you. There is no quick-fix solution to the problem of unrequited love. Yes, you can draw amour to you in various forms, but you cannot make the Jude Law lookalike from accounts fall into your arms at the drop of a hat. It just won't happen, unless it is meant to happen (and then you *are* a very lucky lady!). Free will must be allowed in all things. It is far better to list the qualities of your ideal man and focus on drawing these into your life. You can ask for him to be a handsome hunk, but it might not necessarily be the particular handsome hunk you have your eye on at the time! I usually find that fate has other ideas, and ultimately knows best in these situations. It sounds very trite, but it's certainly true that everything happens for a reason.

With this in mind I've included a variety of love spells, from finding love to keeping it, from losing love to pepping up a flagging sex life. Spells for marriage and divorce are also included. Again, these cannot be used to manipulate a situation or other people, but they can help the process move along in a positive way.

So, take a deep breath and tap into your emotions because love is in the air…

Useful common ingredients

- Honey
- Sugar
- Rose (petals and oil)
- Basil

- Rosemary
- Orange (juice, oil or skin)
- Strawberries
- Raspberries
- Tomatoes
- Apples
- Cloves
- Cinnamon sticks
- Cardamom pods
- Mint
- Ylang ylang oil
- Patchouli oil

Spell-casting tips

These are techniques you can try in order to help your spells along, things that you can incorporate into your everyday routine.

Affirmations

Affirmations, like the words used in spells, can be very powerful. Always speak them in the present tense as if what you want is already happening for you. An affirmation to draw a soulmate, for example, would be:

'I have my soulmate' or *'I draw my true love.'*

Repeat these affirmations as often as you can, in your head or out loud. Use them when you have moments of doubt to quieten the chatter in your head and reinforce what you want.

Rose water

Rose water is often used in love spells. To heighten your chances of drawing love, use it every day. Rinse your hands in it, sprinkle or spray it on your clothes, and use it in the bath.

Rose quartz

A beautiful pale pink crystal, this stone is said to attract love and romance. Carry a piece in your handbag.

Pinking

'Pinking' is a visualisation technique that generates some lovely warm feelings and draws people to you. If you are in a room and you want to attract some attention, try to visualise the entire room, all its contents and the people in it completely covered in pink goo. I know this sounds very strange, but it works! Imagine everyone and everything smothered in pink. That's all you have to do. The effects from this are rather amazing. Pink has romantic loving associations, and the act of visualisation will generate that energy around you and within the room.

Hair

In folklore it is believed that a person's hair can be used in love spells. Of course, it's not always easy to get hold of a strand of hair from the object of your affection, and attempting to could get you in a lot of trouble! However, if you do happen to come across an idle strand of his hair, the claim is that if you hold it in running water, you will eventually wear away his resistance. Be aware though that this could be construed as manipulation!

Spells for drawing love and affection

1. A love charm

Ingredients: Clove, cinnamon stick, piece of rose quartz, red or pink drawstring bag or pouch

Best day: Friday

Moon phase: Waxing – for best results perform this spell on or around a new Moon.

Place the clove, cinnamon and rose quartz in the drawstring bag. Spit into the pouch to seal the spell. You may choose to say some words as you are doing this, while visualising yourself being surrounded by pink light, for example:

I draw true love, I draw it near.
I draw the one that I hold dear.

 2. A love bath

Ingredients: Honey, pink or red rose petals (fresh or dried), and rose or patchouli oil

Best day: Friday or Monday

Moon phase: Waxing, so any time leading up to a full Moon

Run a bath while visualising yourself as a goddess drawing admiring glances and attention. You may also choose to think about the kind of person you would like to attract. Add to your bath a spoonful of honey, which is ruled by the goddess Oshun.

Add a handful of rose petals, and finally a couple of drops of scented oil or rose water. (Rose essential oil is good for love; patchouli is an excellent choice to increase sex appeal.) Now all you need to do is soak in the bath, breathe in the lovely aroma and think positive, loving thoughts. The magic will envelope you and brighten your aura.

3. Candle magic to draw a soulmate

Ingredients: Pink candle, paper and pen, sugar

Best day: Friday

Moon phase: On the night of a new or full Moon

After preparing yourself and some space for magical work, light the candle. Sprinkle the sugar around the base of the candle (you may also put some around the wick). Take the paper and pen and write down a list of all the attributes your ideal partner would have. You can be as specific as you like, from physical details to personality traits. Build up a clear picture of this person in your mind's eye. Remember while you are doing this to visualise love coming into your life. Picture it; picture yourself – how you would look and feel when this happens. Finally you may want to say a few words to seal the spell, something like:

I draw my soulmate into my world.
My heart's true match shall be unfurled.
Goddess bless me, make this true,
Through the loving power of you.
So mote it be.

Now take the paper, fold it three times, and burn it in the flame of the candle.

4. To visualise your true love

This spell does not require any ingredients. Although it's best performed on a Friday when the Moon is full, you can do it any time and anywhere. Again, this involves thinking very carefully about what you want from a partner. Think about every kind of attribute – you may want to start with a list and then build up a picture in your head. The most important thing to visualise is yourself happy and loved. Let those wonderful warm feelings fill you up, and imagine that they light you from the inside out. See your aura glowing brightly, and know that as you do so, your aura is increasing in warmth and drawing the right person to you.

Remember, visualisation is about belief: for it to work you have to put yourself in the picture. You have to feel things as if they are really happening. You have to see things in the present to draw them to you. It's a skill which requires practice, but it's incredibly effective once you have mastered it. Try this visualisation every day during the period of a waxing Moon to see positive results.

5. *Visualisation for free-flowing love*

To accept love into your life, you have to be ready for it. A lot of people think they are ready for it because they *want* it, but that's not necessarily the case. Subconsciously they are often afraid of love and this can cause them to put obstacles in the way, or the fear can act as a barrier when they are trying to attract someone. To be sure you are open and ready to attract love, try this visualisation spell.

Ingredients: White candles, scented oils of your choice (lavender and geranium are good for relaxing and balancing emotions)
Best day: Any
Moon phase: Any

Light some white candles, burn scented oils. Focus on your breathing; slow it right down and imagine that as you breathe in, you breathe in light and love, and on your outward breath you let go of any negativity and anxiety. Continue to do this until you feel totally relaxed.

When you reach this point, draw your attention to your chest. Visualise a small glowing ball of pink light in the centre of this space; see it floating there. Feel the warmth inside; feel it reaching out to every part of your body.

Now imagine that the ball of light is a small flower with its petals closed in. Slowly picture the flower unfurling – each petal stretching open to reveal the bright light at the centre.

When the flower is completely open, imagine that the light is getting brighter, extending outwards until it fills your entire chest, until it fills your torso. Now imagine that the light is seeping from the pores in your skin, extending out of your body and into the world. See yourself as a ball of loving pink light. Take some deep breaths and revel in that feeling of love.

When you are ready, return your attention to your breathing, remembering to breathe in light and let go of any anxiety.

Note down any impressions you had during your visualisation. These things may not mean anything to you just now, but might be relevant in the future.

Spells for keeping love strong

1. Love keepsake box

Ingredients: Box of some kind, a piece of your hair and a piece of your lover's, mementos from your relationship, red ribbon
Best day: Friday, but any day will work well with the right intention
Moon phase: Waxing and waning work equally well, as this is a spell about strength and protection

Fill the box with the mementos. These can be anything from photographs, little notes, tickets from places that you have been to together, anything that reminds you of each other and the things you have shared. If you can, place a lock of your hair and one of your lover's in the box. Tie the box with red ribbon and say the following:

My love and I, we are as one. Bound together we are strong. Protect

our love and keep it safe. So mote it be.

Keep the box in a safe place and add items to it whenever you can to refresh the spell.

✱ 2. Love pie

Ingredients: Pastry, cooking apples, strawberries, sugar
Best day: Friday
Moon phase: Waxing

Baking or cooking is as much about magic as it is culinary skill. When you create something to eat, you have an intention in mind. You want it to taste a certain way, have an effect on the people eating it, as well as being nutritious. You have this in mind as you choose your ingredients, and while preparing your dish you are most likely thinking about the end result – how it should look and taste. This is just like putting a spell together, so it makes perfect sense that whenever you cook something for your partner or family, you include a little magic in the mix.

Pies have long been thought of as magical, particularly round pies, although the actual pastry and shape are not as important as what goes into the pie. Here you can mix and match and find ingredients to suit your magical needs. To bake a love pie, make sure you use sweet fruits such as apples and strawberries (both long renowned for their association with love) and, if you want to add a touch of playfulness to your relationship, raspberries.

Follow a basic pie-making recipe, you can even use ready-made pastry to make this easier. Visualise you and your partner eating the pie, your love growing stronger with every mouthful. In fact, as the pie is cooking, visualise the bond of love between you getting stronger, warmer and much more tasty!

✵ 3. Perfection potion

Wine is often used in magic to celebrate and honour the goddess. It is usually drunk at the end of a ritual, and can be used to seal a spell. This simple potion can be made with the magical intention of helping love grow to perfection. It includes the use of cinnamon, which promotes magical success, and oranges, which promote true and spiritual love.

Ingredients: Wine (preferably red), cinnamon, oranges
Best day: Any
Moon phase: Waxing or waning

Heat some red wine in a pan, add a couple of pinches of cinnamon and squeeze in some fresh orange juice. Stir gently while visualising your love strengthening. Serve the wine to your loved one with a slice of orange.

✵ 4. Prevention powder

This spicy mixture is said to help prevent a loved one straying.

Ingredients: Cumin and turmeric
Best day: Any
Moon phase: Waning, or during the dark of the Moon

Mix together equal spoonfuls of cumin and turmeric, then sprinkle the powder inside your lover's shoes.

✵ 5. Candle spell to ease heartache

A broken heart is something that most people suffer from at some point in their life, and it's a pain that can take a long time to heal. This spell doesn't promise to take all that pain away, but it is a very powerful visualisation that can help to sever emotional constraints and aid the process of healing.

Ingredients: White candle, geranium oil, paper and pen
Best day: Any
Moon phase: Waning or during the dark of the Moon, considered a healing time

Sprinkle a couple of drops of geranium oil onto the candle and then light it. Next take a piece of paper, and write your former partner's name on it. Place the paper in the flame and say the following:

Burn away the name, take away the pain.
For the ties that bind are now left behind.
And my heart is healed from the inside out.
So mote it be.

Now sit on the floor as the candle burns and close your eyes. Focus on your breathing, and quieten your mind. Picture yourself and your partner standing in a room. Between you extending from the area just below your breastbone and above the navel is a cord that stretches, connecting you together. Look at this cord. What is it made of? It might be rope or string, or steel or iron. It depends on the type of relationship you had and the effect it had on you (the stronger the cord, the stronger the influence and effect).

Now, on the floor you see a pair of scissors. These are magical scissors that can cut through anything. Pick them up and cut through the cord that attaches you to this person. As you do so, say, *'I release you and me.'*

When you have finished, feel your body float away, no longer trapped by any emotional attachments.

Spells for marriage and divorce

1. Candle spell to encourage a marriage proposal

Warning: There is no 100 per cent guarantee that this spell will encourage a proposal, and there's no limit on the time this will take. As with any spell, you have to allow for free will, but if it is meant to be in both hearts, this spell will promote a strong sense of unity between you and your partner and encourage the flow and progression of love.

Ingredients: Two pink candles, pin, rose water or rose petals, rose essential oil
Best day: Friday
Moon phase: Waxing, in particular the night of the new Moon as this lends itself to supporting new ventures

While thinking of your loved one, inscribe his name into one of the candles, and yours into the other. Anoint both candles with rose oil and surround them with rose petals. You could also place a vase of red or pink roses nearby as you perform your spell. Rinse your hands in rose water to heighten the power.

Light both candles and stare into the flames. Now visualise your loved one asking you to marry him. See the picture as vividly as possible. Imagine how you will feel. Let your emotions take over and chant the following:

My love and I, we are as one.
Our love it grows forever strong
And we are bound together in life
For I am meant to be his wife.
So mote it be.

Now let the candles burn down.

✦ 2. For a magical marriage

You can create a marriage keepsake box (as with the love keepsake box earlier) to keep a marriage strong and happy.

You can also use animal magic to promote a long and happy marriage. Ducks are said to mate for life, and so it is considered lucky to have images of ducks in your home. You can do this with other creatures too. Swans and wolves, for example, also mate for life, so use images of these creatures around the home and in your keepsake box.

✦ 3. Justice spell for a smooth divorce

This spell is not complicated, but does mean obtaining special ingredients. You can order Mandrake and High John Conqueror roots from specialist suppliers (see suggestions at the end of the book). The Justice tarot card is also used in this spell. If you want to explore the tarot and its magical symbolism, it makes sense to have two packs – one for divination and a disposable one that you can use for your magical work.

Ingredients: Justice tarot card, Mandrake root, High John Conqueror root, black drawstring pouch or bag
Best day: Wednesday or Thursday
Moon phase: Waxing, preferably around the time of the new or full Moon

The primary meaning of the Justice card is, as you might expect, justice and fairness in legal matters. It's a card of balance and honesty.

Take the Justice card and focus on the matter in hand. Think about the qualities of the card and how you would like them to affect your divorce. Take the Mandrake and High John Conqueror roots and burn them in a bowl. Let the smoke drift about you.

Next burn the Justice card over the bowl until all the ash is mixed with the herbs. Fill your drawstring pouch with the ash and herbs.

Keep the pouch about your person as a charm during any legal meetings or court visits related to your divorce.

Spells for sex and fertility

1. Spicy love cocktail

The fruits in this spell have particular romantic properties: raspberries and blueberries have a flirtatious sexy nature, mango gives the body and soul a power boost, and strawberries induce love and romance. Mint is also a wonderful herb for love spells.

Ingredients: Strawberries, raspberries, blueberries, mango, fresh mint, sugar
Best day: Any day you hope to spice up your love life
Moon phase: Waxing

This is very simple. Take the fruits and blend them with some ice. Serve in sugar-rimmed glasses (remember, sugar is a strong attractor in love spells). Add some mint leaves to the finished drink. As you blend the ingredients together, visualise yourself and your lover sharing the cocktail and any intimate moments that might follow.

2. Lusty lavender underwear spell

This is a very old but simple spell based on folklore.

Ingredients: Lavender oil and your favourite underwear
Best day: Any
Moon phase: Any

Sprinkle a couple of drops of lavender essential oil onto your underwear. This is said to make the wearer irresistible!

3. Sexy love bath

This powerful cocktail stimulates romantic and erotic thoughts and is said to free you of your inhibitions.

Ingredients: Hibiscus petals (dried), thyme leaves, vanilla extract (optional)
Best day: Friday, or any evening when love is in the air
Moon phase: Waxing, if possible

Make an infusion by adding hot water to the hibiscus petals and thyme leaves, and add it to your bath water, or that of your lover. The thyme infusion is said to make a person irresistible.

Vanilla extract also has powerful and sexy properties, so, for an extra boost, add a couple of drops to your infusion.

4. Sexy soup

This soup is tasty, should leave you bursting with vitality, and includes ingredients to promote love and lust. Tomatoes are often referred to as the 'love apple', and they happen to be healthy too. Carrots are associated with male fertility and prowess.

Ingredients: Chopped tomatoes, carrots and onion; fresh basil; salt and pepper; olive oil; a little cream
Best day: Your next intimate dinner for two
Moon phase: Any

Fry the onion in a little olive oil. Add the carrots and some boiling water. Mix in the chopped tomatoes. Blend the mixture then return to the pan, add a little salt and pepper to taste and a splash of cream.

Garnish with fresh basil (an excellent herb for drawing love and abundance). Serve with a smile!

5. Fertility salad

Nuts, pulses and seeds are all associated with fertility magic, so include lots of them in this salad. Cucumber is also linked with fertility and virility. Lettuce has relaxing connotations. The tomatoes, red onion and mustard will add colour, spice and a little magic!

Ingredients: Nuts, pulses, seeds (sesame and pumpkin), cucumber, lettuce, baby/cherry tomatoes, red onion, French mustard dressing
Best day: Any
Moon phase: Waxing

Simply make a salad by combining the above ingredients, finishing with a French mustard dressing. You can make your own dressing by mixing a dab of wholegrain mustard in some extra virgin olive oil. While you are preparing the salad, be sure to visualise yourself pregnant, and hold the image in your mind as you eat.

6. Baby altar visualisation

As mentioned in Chapter 2, you can create an altar to support a specific magical need. In the case of fertility, it is definitely worth taking the time to create a special altar and adorn it with ornaments and pictures that support your aim. Trying to conceive a baby can be a long and complicated process and the fact that you are considering a spell suggests that there might have been some difficulties. Therefore, you want to give your magic the best chance of working.

Seeds and nuts are an excellent choice as an offering to the goddess for fertility, as well as being nutritious to eat. Leave a bowl upon your altar, along with fresh flowers, and any pictures or ornaments you feel are appropriate. Make sure you change the flowers regularly; the idea being that you are promoting new growth.

Ingredients: Altar; various baby items; appropriate images (pictures or ornaments); seeds; green candle; geranium, rose or lavender oil
Best day: Any, but Mondays are especially good for women's health problems as they are ruled by the Moon
Moon phase: Waxing, as you want to encourage new growth

Try this simple visualisation sitting before your altar. Anoint the green candle with oil by rubbing the oil lengthways into the candle. As you light the candle, perform this simple visualisation.

Take a deep breath in, then, as you breathe out, imagine that you are purging your body of all the negative toxins that have built up over the years. As you breathe in again, imagine that you are filling your body with health and vitality, that a stream of pure white light warms you from the inside out. Continue to concentrate on your breathing until you feel calm and relaxed.

Place your hands on your tummy and feel the warmth, the healing energy, passing through your skin into your uterus. Now imagine that you are sitting in the middle of a beautiful meadow. The sun is shining and there are flowers everywhere. You can hear the birds singing. You feel a faint breeze on your face. You can smell the sweet scent of the flowers. The grass is soft beneath you as you relax. You look down and notice that you are wearing a dress. It feels like silk. As you look closely, you notice there are flowers everywhere in the fabric.

You stroke the ground with your fingers and as you do so, small green saplings rise out of the ground and begin to blossom. You realise then that you have the power to create new life. You are like

Mother Earth, loving and nurturing.

Focus on your hands on your stomach and feel a tingling sensation inside. You know that there is new life growing inside you and it is a wonderful feeling. You bask in the glory of the sunshine, and let thoughts of happiness and joy wash over you.

When you are ready, begin once more to focus on your breathing, making sure that you release all the negativity within. As you open your eyes, stare into the flame of the candle and say:

I am Woman, Goddess and Nurturer of all things. I have the power to create new life. I am pregnant.

Practise this visualisation every week using the same candle. It will increase your chances of getting pregnant, and will also make you feel positive, invigorated and brimming with vitality.

7. Baby charm

This is a powerful protection charm to keep negative influences away.

Ingredients: Salt, cloves, garlic, black pouch, piece of silver jewellery (optional)
Best day: Any
Moon phase: Waning

Place a pinch of salt, a clove and a piece of garlic into a black drawstring pouch (you might also like to add a piece of silver) and seal them with saliva. You may also choose to say a few words of protection. Hang the pouch above the baby's cot.

Spells for money, good fortune and success

Lady Luck has much to answer for. She bestows her generous gifts on some, while totally ignoring others, but that's the turning of the wheel of fortune, the wheel of life. Sometimes everything goes our way, then, just when we're settling into our new-found success, something sends us plunging to the depths of despair. Change is the secret to life. Nothing stays the same. It's the one guarantee we have when things are really bad, and in a way that's a comfort.

Magically, there is much we can do to alter the balance of the scales and help things go in our favour, but it has to be said that a positive outlook has much to do with the way things work out. A positive person will seek the best out of a dire situation. A negative person will see the limitations in something which is essentially good. So before you begin any success magic take a look at yourself. Ask yourself these questions – am I a positive person? Is my glass half full or half empty? Like attracts like when it comes to energy and form, so people who are positive are like beacons of light, they attract good things. Those who spend their life concentrating on the negative and focusing on their problems will draw more troubles to their door.

The following spells will encourage the flow of good fortune into your life. They promote success and draw money and prosperity.

Useful common ingredients

- Basil
- Rosemary
- Galangal root
- Vervain
- Bay leaves
- Dill
- Ginger
- Cinnamon
- Cloves
- Nutmeg
- Frankincense
- Orange
- Fools gold
- Lodestone
- Amber
- Bamboo

Spell-casting tips

Rain

In folklore, the first rain in spring is said to have particularly lucky properties. When it looks like rain, take a container outside and collect some then use the water to wash or bathe in. This will supposedly bless you with a year of good luck.

Tin

Tin is the metal most associated with good luck. Make your own lucky charm by cutting a shape out of tin and inscribing it. Keep it with you in a drawstring bag. You can add various herbs and oils to the bag too, to increase the potency of this spell. Horseshoes have always been considered incredibly lucky, so if you can, cut the tin into the shape of a horseshoe and carry this with you.

Pineapple

Pineapple juice is said to bring joy and good fortune in abundance. Drink it and add it to magical baths with basil and rose petals.

Mistletoe

This plant is said to be lucky, and not only in the kissing department! Tie sprigs of mistletoe together and hang them about your house to inspire luck and romance.

Basil and Rosemary

Distribute pots of growing basil about your house to encourage the flow of money and prosperity in your home. Rosemary is also a powerful herb, particularly for women. If you want to feel more powerful and in control of your life, and particularly if you want to instigate some action, grow some rosemary in your garden; the bigger the bush, the stronger the influence and magic.

⊛ 1. Charm for good luck

This particular charm was created with a man in mind, but the tiger's eye stone can be substituted for adventurine to work equally well for a woman. It works well when someone is taking an exam or test of any kind.

Ingredients: Green drawstring bag, piece of tiger's eye, cinnamon stick, nutmeg (oil or powder)
Best day: Sunday, the day of glory and fulfilment
Moon phase: Waxing

Fill the pouch with the stone, cinnamon and nutmeg. If you are using oil, a couple of drops will be enough. As you do so, visualise the person who is taking the test, see them telling you they've passed. Feel their joy. You may choose to say a few words to seal the spell. Give the person the charm bag and tell them to keep it with them during the test.

2. Easy success spell

The key to success is the right attitude and having an unwavering belief in your abilities. It's also a little luck, being in the right place at the right time and having those opportunities land at your feet. The following is a simple success spell that can work on anything, whether it's planning an evening with the family or setting up a business venture.

Ingredients: High John Conqueror root (you can get this at a herbal supply shop or from the internet), frankincense, gold or yellow candle, paper and pen
Best day: Thursday
Moon phase: Waxing

Light the candle and begin to think about your magical needs. Visualise yourself achieving your goal. How does it feel to be a success? Think about that for a moment. Then write down your goal on the paper. Place the High John Conqueror root and the frankincense in a bowl and let it burn. Frankincense lifts the vibrations of a place and is great when asking for wish fulfilment.

Take the paper with your magical wish and hold it in the flame, still visualising your success. Then toss the paper in the bowl with the burning frankincense and herbs (you can add other success herbs to the mix if you wish). Say the following words:

Everything I touch turns to gold.
What I reap returns to me threefold.
I am blessed with success in all that I do.
My aim as I've written has come true.
So mote it be.

If you can get hold of frankincense essential oil, you can also burn this at the same time for maximum impact.

✪ 3. *Prosperity spell*

Ingredients: Three gold candles; salt; £10, £20 or £50 note
Best day: Thursday
Moon phase: Waxing, or full Moon

Arrange the three candles in the shape of a triangle. In the centre, place a note, the highest amount you have. Light the three candles and sprinkle salt around them in the circle. Say the following (or something similar):

Prosperity is mine at this time! (Repeat three times.) *So mote it be.*
Let the candles burn. Repeat the spell every night for a week.

✪ 4. *Candle money spell*

Ingredients: Green candle, cinnamon oil, basil oil (or some fresh leaves if unavailable), paper and pen
Best day: Any
Moon phase: Waxing

Think about the amount of money you would like to draw into your life. Be honest and reasonable. What do you need? What would help you at the moment? Don't be extravagant for the sake of it.

Write the amount on the paper, and draw a circle around it. Next anoint the candle with the oils: cinnamon for success and basil for money. If you can't find any basil oil, rub some basil leaves into the candle and scatter them around the base. Light the candle. Then burn the paper in the flame. Say:

This money is mine. I have it now. So mote it be.

Remember to visualise the money coming to you. Picture yourself with a cheque in your hands. See your face. Imagine how you will feel. Have faith that the spell has worked. If you don't have 100 per cent faith, only part of the spell will work. You might receive a small windfall, but it won't be anywhere near the amount you need.

5. Money bath

Basil is associated with money magic as the leaves are said to resemble notes. Basil also attracts good fortune.

Ingredients: Fresh basil
Best day: Sunday, Wednesday or Thursday
Moon phase: Waxing; for urgent financial assistance try this spell on a new Moon.

Steep some fresh basil in hot water. When you are ready, either strain the basil from the mix and add the infusion to your bath, or throw everything in – either way it has the same effect. As you immerse yourself in the bath, imagine you are immersing yourself in a bath full off money. Feel the money falling from the universe into your lap. You can also imagine you are standing beneath your very own money tree, see the branches shake and watch the money tumble to the ground at your feet. See it all around you and know in your heart that your money worries are over. Repeat the following:

As I see, so mote it be.

✪ 6. *Business development wash*

A floor wash might seem a strange type of spell, but in fact it's a very traditional method of spell-casting because it allows for discreet magic.

Ingredients: Ground cinnamon, citronella oil, basil leaves, white vinegar
Best day: Thursday, ideally, but any day before the start of business
Moon phase: Waxing

Make an infusion of basil leaves, strain and add to hot water. Then add in the cinnamon and a couple of drops of citronella essential oil. Add a splash of white vinegar. Now use the solution to wash the floor of your workplace. Ideally you should also wash the front steps that lead into your business. This will encourage the flow of money and custom into your place of work.

✪ 7. *Success wish*

Ingredients: Choose from cloves to draw good things, cinnamon for general success, rose petals for success in love, depending on your wish.
Best day: Again, this depends up on the type of wish. Success in love would best favour a Friday; success in business a Thursday; success in securing or negotiating any kind of deal would be best favoured on a Wednesday.
Moon phase: Waxing Moon, but for optimum success, a full Moon. Wishes on the night of a full Moon are always blessed.

Stand under the light of the Moon. Hold the ingredients in your hands and offer them up to the light of the Moon. Say:

As the wind blows, then my fate flows.
I now have success, I am truly blessed.
So mote it be.

When you have finished, open your hands, spin around and let the ingredients scatter. Know in your heart and mind that your wish has been heard and will be answered at a time and place that is right for you.

8. Gambling charm

Ingredients: Whole nutmeg (or the powdered form or essential oil)
Best day: Any day when you're going to have a flutter or take a chance
Moon phase: Waxing

This is very simple. Nutmeg is considered the gambler's lucky charm. So the next time you are going to gamble, carry a whole nutmeg in your pocket. If you can't do this, dust your hands with the powdered version while visualising your success, or sprinkle a few drops of the oil onto a handkerchief and carry this in your pocket.

9. Spell for a change in fortune

The idea behind this spell is to get things moving. If you've had a run of bad luck, this spell should help to clear it from your life.

Ingredients: One orange candle, one black candle, small knife
Best day: Tuesday, Thursday, Saturday, Sunday
Moon phase: Waxing, and on a full Moon

The orange candle represents yourself, so carve your initials into it. The black candle represents negative energy currently in your life. Light the black candle and as you do so, think about all the things that have gone wrong; all the things that you would like to rid from your life. Say something like:

I am free from negative energy, it is gone from me.

Now light the orange candle and think about all the good things that you would like to come into your life. Say something like:

Good fortune is mine. I am moving on.

Success is here. Bad luck is gone!

Let the candles burn out and continue to visualise a change in fortune.

✪ 10. The Wheel of Fortune

The Wheel of Fortune is the tarot card associated with change and luck. When the wheel goes up, we are riding high, and life is treating us to all kinds of blessings. When the wheel goes down, however, everything changes and we may have a run of bad luck. One thing is certain with the Wheel of Fortune, nothing stays the same for long and you can expect major change. So it makes sense that if you want to instigate change in your life, and change for the better, you can use the power of this card in your spell work.

The simplest way to do this is to pick out the card from a tarot pack and do a simple visualisation. See the card clearly in your mind, and imagine stepping into it. Imagine that you are riding the wheel just as you would in a fairground. See yourself at the bottom – this is where you are now. Then see yourself rising and your situation improving. Feel the joy and elation of happiness and good fortune and know that it is yours for the taking. You may want to say a few words to seal the spell, but this is not necessary if you have a clear image in your head. Once you reach the top, hold that thought. See that picture, and then let it go; imagine it drifting away into the universe.

Step out of the card and back into your mind and your everyday life.

If you don't have a pack of tarot cards, just picture a big wheel in your head and see it as the wheel of life, the wheel that controls your fortune. It's the significance of this image that is the most important thing.

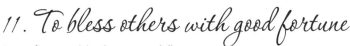

11. To bless others with good fortune

Ingredients: Elder leaves and flowers

Best day: Any day you are feeling benevolent!

Moon phase: Waxing

Find a wide open space outside, perhaps your garden or a local park. Gather the leaves and flowers in your hands, hold them and spin around while saying:

I bless [person's name] with all my might.

May Lady Fortune have them in her sight!

Open your hands and scatter the leaves and flowers, as if you are scattering the gifts of happiness and good fortune.

CHAPTER EIGHT

Spells for work and career

Whether you go out to work, or your work is in the house, it still takes up a large part of the day. We all have to work to achieve the things we want; it's a fact of life. Sometimes that work is easy, and sometimes it's an uphill struggle to fit everything in. Sometimes we encounter difficult people, or we don't feel we are getting the recognition we deserve. But work need not be stressful, and the following spells should help with everyday chores and work issues.

Useful common ingredients

- Coffee
- Bread
- Rice
- Ice
- Cloves
- Garlic
- Rosemary
- Basil
- Onion

- Yellow flowers of any kind
- Jasmine (dried or fresh)

1. A good working environment

This is more of a magical recommendation than an actual spell, and it really does work.

Ingredients: Fresh coffee, daffodils (or any yellow flower)

The smell of fresh coffee brewing has a magical positive effect on the mind. It stimulates the senses and motivates people; therefore it makes sense to keep a pot of coffee brewing in a working environment. Also keep a fresh vase of yellow flowers in the area. Daffodils in particular attract friendly spirits to a place, but any yellow flower promotes happy feelings of cooperation. You can also try this in your home.

Having problems with a colleague? Soothe troubled waters with a bunch of yellow roses. If nothing else, it will be a lovely gesture and a surprise. Never underestimate the element of surprise! When you hand over any gift, use the moment to implant positive suggestions. If you're trying to heal a rift, say in your head as you give your gift, 'We are friends, and everything is fine.'

2. To get a pay rise

There are two versions of this spell, using either bread or rice. The general idea is that the act of baking bread or cooking a pot of rice can help magically with growth of any kind, but particularly the finances.

Ingredients: Bread mix and bread maker or rice
Best day: Wednesday
Moon phase: Waxing
Either make some bread in the conventional way, or with a bread

maker. As you do so visualise your pay packet growing. If you don't eat bread, try a similar visualisation with a pot of rice – as the rice expands and soaks up the water, imagine your finances increasing. See your bank balance swell.

Then make an appointment with your boss on a Wednesday, ask Mercury to bless your communication skills, and negotiate that pay rise!

✦ 3. To freeze out the competition

This spell helps you to block out any negative influences and works particularly well with vindictive people in the work place (or any place for that matter!).

Ingredients: Paper and pen, ice

Write down the name of the person who has been causing you problems. Screw up the paper, place it in an ice cube container and fill this with water. You can also use an ice bag or box. Put it in the freezer. Imagine that the person's influence upon you is frozen; they no longer have any affect on you or your work. See them motionless, behind a sheet of ice. This spell frees you from any kind of manipulation.

✦ 4. Help with power struggles at work (and play)

Ingredients: Onion
Best day: Tuesday

If you find yourself head to head with a colleague, or in any situation where there is opposition, ask Mars for help on a Tuesday. Mars is the planet of battle and can help when there are power struggles or you need to assert yourself. Onions are associated with Mars and can dispel negative energy. As you peel an onion, see the opposition dwindling; see the power they have fading. Now see yourself taking control of the situation; see your victory and believe it!

5. Charm for the job of your dreams

Lodestones are nature's magnets. They draw things to you. If you cannot get hold of a lodestone, a crystal can be used. Quartz crystal is a good all-rounder, or you might choose a stone that reflects the kind of job you want. For instance, a blue stone like lapis lazuli or turquoise is associated with creativity and communication. Rose quartz is the heart stone and a wonderful gem for anyone in the caring profession. Amethyst opens up intuition and helps to develop psychic skills. Find a good book on the subject and investigate the type of stone that would work best for you.

Note: Stones and crystals can be charged for any specific purpose, and you might have a number of charms for different aims.

Ingredients: Lodestone, green candle
Best day: Monday or Wednesday
Moon phase: Waxing

Light a green candle and visualise the type of job that you want while holding the stone in your hand. Consider all the things that you want this job to be. What kind of tasks do you enjoy doing? Where will the job be? How many hours do you want to work? What would you like to be paid? See yourself doing the job. When you have a clear picture, hold the stone up to your lips, take a deep breath, then imagine that, through your outward breath, you are pouring all that information – the image of what you want – into the stone. Say the following:

As I see, I shall be.
As I search, I will find.

So mote it be.

The stone is now magically charged and will act as a charm. It will guide you in your search for that dream job.

✦ 6. *Charm for the business traveller*

The Moon looks down on us wherever we are in the world, so if a loved one is travelling with work, whether in this country or a more exotic location, create this easy traveller's charm.

Ingredients: Piece of Moonstone
Best day: The Monday night before your loved one departs
Moon phase: Waxing, preferably

Take the Moonstone and hold it in your hands under the light of the Moon. Say a few words to help secure the safe return of the person who is travelling. Place the stone under the light of the Moon overnight so that it absorbs the rays. Give it to your loved one to keep in their luggage during the trip.

✦ 7. *Magical protection for travellers*

Here's a simple magical protection technique if you or someone you love is travelling with work.

Ingredients: Compact make-up mirror, clove of garlic, salt

Smear the mirror with the garlic. Now sprinkle the salt on it. Close it up and keep it in your luggage. If you are stopping in a hotel, keep the mirror open under your bed or on a bedside table to deflect any negative energy that might be lurking.

CHAPTER NINE

Spells for home and family

Our home is our castle, so people say. It's certainly the place where we feel most secure, the place where we can be ourselves. We often neglect our home; we rush around getting caught up with everyday chores instead of spending time making it the warm and friendly place it should be. Sometimes our home is under threat through no fault of our own and we would like to protect it. Sometimes we feel our home has been taken over by negativity; maybe there have been too many arguments and the atmosphere feels uncomfortable. These are all problems that can be solved with a little magic.

Useful common ingredients

- Sage
- Thyme
- Rosemary
- Rue
- Vervain
- Pine

- Lavender (flowers or oil)
- Lemon
- Geranium (flowers or oil)
- Daffodil
- Juniper berries
- Cumin
- Onion
- Milk

Spell-casting tips

Hair and nails

Hair cuttings and toenail clippings can be used in magic to keep a family together. Gather either a cutting of hair or nail clippings from each member of the family. Put these in a small drawstring pouch, or wrap them in pink or white cloth, and then bury it at the bottom of your garden. This is said to keep your family unit tight and in harmony.

Oil

Olive oil absorbs negativity. Mix a few drops of olive oil with lavender essential oil to promote happy feelings. Dab this on the exact spot where a confrontation has occurred, to clear away any negative feelings.

As a relaxing alternative, and to help heal any rifts, make a mixture of olive oil (almond or sunflower oil can also be used) with lavender and use it as a massage oil for your partner. It's a nice gesture and the oils will work their magic and improve communication.

Salt

In folklore it was believed that if you tossed salt into your cooking fire every week, it would keep your family happy and protected.

Blue and white

Blue and white are colours that promote peace and tranquillity. Wherever possible, burn candles of this colour around the house.

1. Negativity cleanse

This is a very simple spell to cleanse any area of negativity. You might want to do this in the room or space that you use for your magical work.

Ingredients: Sage leaves, rosemary

Take a bowl of sage leaves and some rosemary. Burn them if they are dried, or steep them in hot water if they are fresh. Let the vapours or smoke drift around all the corners of the room, and visualise the room being cleared of any heavy unwanted energies.

Alternatively you can make a simple floor wash with these herbs and the additions of a splash of lemon juice, some pine oil and hot water. Not only does it freshen up the floor surface and have a lovely smell, it will cleanse the area.

2. To protect your home

Ingredients: Juniper berries, onion

It is believed in folklore that juniper berries can scare away unwanted intruders. So, if you feel your home is under threat, hang some juniper in the windows, or perhaps place a sprig on your front door.

Onions too are wonderful at warding off unwanted influences. Chop an onion into quarters and place the quarters in north, south, east and west areas inside your home. The onion will drive away any negativity.

✪ 3. *For a happy home*

Everyone wants a happy home and there are things you can do as a home-maker and a witch to promote those feelings of cooperation!

Ingredients: Lavender oil, daffodils or yellow roses, rue (herb or oil)

Begin by casting a circle and inviting white light to flood your home and fill it with positive and protective energies.

Heat some lavender oil, as this promotes relaxation and happiness. Place a vase of yellow flowers on your altar or in your living room.

Burn some rue and imagine any awkward problems and barriers to communication disappearing in the smoke. If you like, say a few words to reinforce your magical aim:

Spirits of the north, south, east and west,
Keep this happy home safe and blessed.
So mote it be.

Let the lavender and rue burn out, infusing the house with warm and loving vibrations.

✪ 4. *To find your dream home*

This spell is quite similar in format to the spell to attract a soulmate, but it uses charm magic rather than candles. It involves thinking very carefully about and listing your needs.

Ingredients: Paper and a pen, picture of the type of house you would like, quartz crystal and/or lodestone, drawstring pouch

Best day: Any

Moon phase: Waxing

List the things that your dream home will have. Make sure you consider everything from the size and the setting, to the preferred price. Be realistic. The universe will provide what you need, depending on what you have. If you're not a millionaire, you won't be offered a three-storey mansion. Place the list and the picture into the pouch along with the crystal and lodestone. The crystal will amplify your needs and give extra energy to your request; the lodestone is a natural magnet and will help to draw this to you. Seal the contents of the charm bag with some spit. Carry the charm with you at all times until your needs are met.

5. Happy home floor wash

This floor wash can be used to promote feelings of happiness in the home. It is particularly good if you work from home as it will draw in business and money.

Ingredients: Either orange or citronella essential oil, lemon juice, white vinegar, basil leaves

Add several drops of your chosen essential oil to a bucket of hot water, along with a couple of drops of lemon juice and white vinegar. Make an infusion of basil leaves, strain the liquid and add it to your floor wash. Clean away any unhappy feelings, and remember to visualise as you go.

6. To banish sadness

Ingredients: White candle, paper and red pen, honey
Best day: Monday
Moon phase: Waning Moon

Light the candle while thinking of all the things in your life that cause you sadness. Take the paper and red pen and list your woes.

When you have done this, drizzle some honey in a circle over the paper. Now take the paper and burn it in the candle flame. Imagine that your worries and sorrows are melting away, leaving only lovely warm healing energies.

CHAPTER TEN

Spells for health and well-being

Good health is vital. It is true that we have nothing if we do not have our health, and yet it's something we often neglect because we lead such busy lives. Simple health problems can develop into more worrying conditions if ignored, but a little magic can help.

Health does not only mean physical health, it means mental, emotional and spiritual well-being too. The following pages include spells to help you on every level from healing physical problems to improving an emotional outlook. There are also spells to help deal with addictions.

Useful common ingredients

- Sage
- Thyme
- Mint
- Rue
- Rose hips
- Rosemary
- Tea tree oil
- Frankincense (incense or oil)

- Lavender
- Ginger
- Mustard
- Honey
- Milk
- Mango
- Lemon
- Lime
- Lemon
- Potato
- Broccoli
- Cabbage
- Eggs

1. To lose weight

There are many spells to help you lose weight or stick to a diet. I have found that this is the most effective, and it's also fun!

Ingredients: Potato, small knife, potato peeler

Best day: Any; it might be helpful to do this every night for a week to start off with.

Moon phase: Waning if possible; the idea is that as the Moon wanes and reduces in size, so will you!

Carve your name into the potato; imagine that the potato represents you as you are. Now begin to peel. As you do this, visualise yourself losing weight, just as the potato is decreasing in size, then say the following words:

I am slim, I am fit,
I am getting rid of it!

You can perform this magical ritual every time you feel tempted to indulge. It will help to focus your mind and keep you occupied should the biscuit tin be calling!

I should add that potatoes have other magical properties to do with health. In the past it was believed that carrying a potato in your pocket could get rid of any muscle or joint pain.

✸ 2. *Sore throat potion*

Sage is excellent for soothing bad throats, and honey is a natural antibiotic. You could also try a similar infusion with slippery elm, thyme and rose hips. They all have strong medicinal properties.

Ingredients: Fresh sage leaves, honey (Manuka if possible), a lemon
Best day: Any day you have a sore throat! Or when the Sun or Moon is in Taurus, as this sign governs the throat and neck.
Moon phase: Waning, if possible, as you want to reduce the inflammation

Steep a handful of sage leaves in hot water for a few minutes, then strain. Add a teaspoon of honey and a few drops of freshly squeezed lemon juice, and drink. As you do so, visualise the liquid sliding down your throat and coating it in a warm protective layer.

✸ 3. *Potion to lift your spirits*

It's not always easy to lift your spirits, but this spell can provide a magical pick me up and put a bounce to your step! The magical properties of each fruit will give you an energy boost as well as cleansing the system in preparation for the day.

Ingredients: Fresh mango, a lime, lemon juice
Best day: Any, in the morning
Moon phase: Any

Peel and juice the mango, cut the lime in half and squeeze the juice into the mixture, and add a dash of lemon juice. Drink this first thing in the morning.

In addition, you can take some of the mango skin and carve your magical wish into it, leave it to dry on your window sill and then carry it as a lucky charm. If you feel you need a power boost, write words to that effect on the skin and keep it with you. Mango has strong protective qualities. Carve your initials into the skin and keep it in a drawstring pouch as a talisman.

✷ 4. Immune booster snack

There is no quick fix for an weak immune system; it takes time, a healthy diet and exercise. There are, however, certain foods and herbs that have magical properties which can strengthen your immune system, especially if you use them in conjunction with visualisation. Broccoli is known for its protective elements, and peas were once considered a staple of the witch's diet. Peas are also an excellent source of vitamin C. Garlic has always been associated with protection, and cheese has nurturing properties.

Ingredients: Broccoli, peas, clove of garlic, Parmesan cheese
Best day: Any
Moon phase: Waxing, if possible, to help you draw strength and good health

Steam the broccoli and peas, add a clove of garlic, and once cooked sprinkle with Parmesan cheese. Serve as a light lunch or starter.

Alternatively, why not make a soup from the broccoli, peas and garlic? Just cook and blend all the ingredients together, then sprinkle the Parmesan cheese over the steaming soup and enjoy!

Remember while cooking to visualise and focus your intention. See the energy in the food; imagine there's a blue healing light surrounding the vegetables.

5. *Magical bath fit for a goddess*

Ingredients: Honey, rose petals, milk, lavender essential oil
Best day: Friday
Moon phase: Waxing, if possible

To feel a million dollars try this simple magical bath. Mix a couple of teaspoons of honey in a glass of warm milk and add this to the running water of your bath. Then take a handful of rose petals of any colour and scatter them in the water. Finally add a couple of drops of lavender. As you immerse yourself in the scented depths, visualise yourself as a goddess, adored and worshipped by many. Say the following affirmation:

I am desirable, gorgeous and sweet –
I have men and women falling at my feet.

You may also want to repeat this affirmation while applying body cream or moisturiser. Introduce it into your beauty regime until it becomes a natural part of bathing and second nature. Let that goddess shine every day!

6. *Tea for mental clarity*

This is an excellent potion to drink before you take a test or exam, or when you find yourself in a situation where you must stay alert. It's very easy to make too.

Rosemary is a wonderful herb to awaken the senses and restore mental clarity. It's a herb that promotes feminine strength, so you can drink an infusion whenever you want to boost your personal power. If you have an important event coming up where you need to charm people, use this tea along with visualisation and a few words to hone your intentions on a Wednesday. Ask Mercury to help enhance your communication skills and keep your mind alert and agile.

Ingredients: Sprig of rosemary, mint leaves, honey
Best day: Any
Moon phase: Any

Steep the sprig of rosemary and the mint leaves in hot water for a few minutes, add a spoonful of honey, and drink. It's as simple as that!

✪ 7. *Headache relief*

Ingredients: Smooth stone
Best day: Whenever required!
Moon phase: Any

This easy spell requires a little visualisation. All you need is a clean stone from the garden. Rub the stone along your forehead and imagine that all the badness, pain and tension is being absorbed by the stone. Feel it being drawn from your forehead. Do this for a few minutes. When you are ready, take the stone back into your garden and bury it deep within the soil. The Earth will absorb and transform the negative energies.

You can do a similar magical exercise with an egg. Roll the egg over your forehead as above and imagine that it is pulling the pain from you. When you are ready, take the egg, smash it and bury the remains in your garden.

✪ 8. *To heal others*

This is an easy spell that can be used to heal someone from a distance.

Ingredients: Blue candle, small knife
Best day: Any
Moon phase: Any

The blue candle represents the person that you want to help. Blue is used as it is the best colour for healing. Carve the person's name or initials into the candle. Remember to visualise that person getting better as you do this. Light the candle and, as the flame burns, picture the person surrounded by blue light; see the light absorbed into their body, reaching the parts of them that need to be healed. You may choose to say a few words to seal the spell. Repeat this spell on consecutive nights to increase the effects.

9. Healing spell for viruses

Feeling under the weather? The doctor says it's a virus but there's nothing he can give you for it...? Try this spell to encourage a speedy recovery.

Ingredients: Piece of fresh ginger, clove, salt, clove of garlic, square of velvet (or handkerchief), blue thread
Best day: Any
Moon phase: Any

Fill the cloth or handkerchief with the ingredients. Tie it up with the blue thread. Every morning and night inhale deeply and imagine the scent cleansing your entire body of the virus.

10. To alleviate stress and tension

This spell also relies on the power of scent and the healing properties of certain plants and flowers.

Ingredients: Cauldron (or pot or oil burner can also be used), olive oil, lemon juice or oil, rose petals, fresh sage
Best day: Any day you feel stressed!
Moon phase: Any, although a waning Moon is best to reduce the effects of stress

Pour all of the ingredients into your cauldron or pot and heat for five minutes. Close your eyes and inhale the aroma. Do this while visualising a shower of pure white light washing through your body and cleansing it of any tension. If you use an oil burner, leave the ingredients simmering so that the entire room is filled with the relaxing scent.

11. To lift someone's spirits

Ingredients: Daffodils (or other yellow flowers), vase, photograph of the person you want to help
Best day: Friday works particularly well, but you can use this spell any day
Moon phase: Waxing, if possible

Place the person's picture under a vase filled with water. Now add the flowers to the vase. As you do so, visualise a warm golden light surrounding the person. See their face break into a wonderful happy smile. You may choose to say a few words like:

> *Golden flowers warm and bright,*
> *May [person's name] be filled with light.*
> *So mote it be.*

Leave the flowers to blossom over night, and if you can, visit the person the next day and give them the bunch of flowers as a gift; not only will it be a nice surprise, but it will also seal the magic you've put in place.

Charging food and drink with magical energy

It is possible to charge anything you eat or drink with magical energy. This means you can boost the nutritional value of any item for positive effect. Charging food and drink is just like charging a talisman or charm.

The next time you are preparing a meal, take each ingredient by itself and hold it up in your hands as if offering it to the universe. Take a deep breath and visualise a stream of bright light pouring down from above through the crown of your head. As you breathe out, imagine that light is streaming out of your mouth and into the food. As you do this say:

I charge you with energy, vitality and health!

You can do the same thing when the meal is ready: just hold your hands over the food and imagine the light pouring from your palms and imbuing the dish with good, healthy energy. This is such a simple technique, but it's really effective, it even makes the food taste better!

You can also charge food and drink with other magical qualities. If, for example, you need more money flowing into your life, check out the particular ingredients that work well in money spells. Cook a meal using some of these ingredients and when you are done, charge the food with magical energy to increase your cash flow by saying a few words and visualising your aim. The same goes for love, success, creativity... The list is endless and it makes cooking a fun experience too!

CHAPTER ELEVEN

Spells for power, psychic development and protection

These three Ps are very important in magical work. They work together and complement one another. As you develop in magical power and knowledge, you will become more psychically aware. This does have a negative knock-on effect in that, as you become more aware, you are also more sensitive, and this leaves you open to psychic attack. You will pick up on negative energies easily. This can happen without you realising it. As you naturally tune into people you will sense their feelings, physically and emotionally. It is not unusual, as you become adept, to pick up on another's ailments, aches and pains. This happens in close-knit families, or with people who have a strong psychic link such as twins.

I often found when I did tarot readings for people that I would start to pick up on physical characteristics, including any aches and pains someone had at the time of the reading. As you can imagine, this was not fun, especially at the point when I developed horrendous toothache! At the time I didn't realise what was happening, but a more experienced reader pointed out that this was my sensitivity developing and a natural side effect of magical work.

This is where protection comes in. You need to protect yourself, and there are a number of magical ways to do this. You may also want to protect your home, working environment and those close to you.

This chapter suggests spells to help you increase your power, to add extra fire to already existing spells. There are spells that help with psychic development, and finally there are spells and protection techniques to help you nurture yourself and your environment.

Spells for power

Spell-casting tips

Blood and saliva

There are certain bodily fluids that have always been considered magical. As mentioned in Chapter 1, the most potent of these is blood, in particular menstrual blood. Some witches still use menstrual blood in their spells to add extra power. This might be a tad extreme. A lesser version of this would be to carry out spells during your period as this is considered a very powerful time for any woman. The next time you're feeling under the weather and generally grotty because it's that time of the month, remember, you are actually at your most magnificent and awe inspiring!

Saliva is another bodily fluid often used to personalise spells. It's like adding your signature to the spell and is often used in spell bags to seal the magic in. It's also less extreme than using blood!

Rosemary and basil

Keep pots of fresh rosemary about the house and burn the oil to stimulate your female power.

Basil is also said to stimulate personal power. Chew it while visualising success. Burn the oil and use together with rosemary in infusions for your bath.

Liquorice

Liquorice root is often used in power spells because of its commanding properties. Chew on liquorice before an important meeting; it is said to help improve powers of persuasion.

Lemons and limes

These fruits are often associated with strength and power. Lemons tend to draw things, and are often used in potent love spells.

Lime juice can also be used to pack a powerful punch and to attract attention. Lime juice tends to stir things up, and can have quite an erratic effect, so use sparingly. Some witches believe that using lime oil can have a souring effect, particular on relationships, so bear that in mind.

✦ 1. Power punch

Ingredients: Mango, lemon juice, sparkling water, ground ginger
Best day: Any day when you want your personal power to shine through
Moon phase: Waxing

Peel the mango and chop it into small pieces. Blend the mango with some freshly squeezed lemon juice and half a glass of sparkling water. Add a couple of pinches of ginger to the mix and drink. As you drink, visualise your aura shining brightly. This is best drunk first thing in the morning to cleanse and invigorate the system!

✦ 2. Rosemary charm

Rosemary is the women's herb and is great to use as an infusion or tea for mental clarity and strength of mind. It can be used alongside rue as a charm.

Ingredients: Rosemary sprig, rue (if you have it), lemon oil, small bag
Best day: Monday, ruled by the Moon and a good day for female power
Moon phase: Waxing, in particular around the time of a full Moon

Take a sprig of fresh rosemary, a sprinkling of the dried herb rue, and add to a small spell bag or pouch. Add a couple of drops of lemon essential oil or fresh lemon oil, then spit into the bag to seal the spell. Say the following:

Power is mine. Power is strong.
My strength as a woman goes on and on.
Mother Moon she casts her glow,
Upon this night, my powers grow.
So mote it be.

Keep the charm bag with you at all times. You can refresh the bag at any time to keep the power strong.

Power oil

A power oil is a scented oil that you prepare using ingredients that resonate with you. It's an oil that is unique to you, and is used to increase the power of your spells. You can either use power oils directly in spells, for example anointing candles with the oil, or use it in potions. You can also apply the oil to your body and hands before you do any magical work for an extra boost. If you make plenty of the oil, you can decant it into handbag-sized bottles to keep with you and use whenever you need to increase your personal power.

General ingredients for power oils differ because it is a personal thing. There is always a base oil, and this must be something that you can use on skin without irritation. I suggest almond oil, although sunflower and olive oil are fine too. Sunflower is an excellent oil to use on men. It's directly linked to the strong male energy of the Sun.

Think about what kind of qualities you would like to inspire. Which qualities will help you increase your magical powers?

- Cinnamon, orange and nutmeg essential oils promote success, the ability to make your own luck and strength.
- Patchouli, ylang ylang, mint and rose inspire love and attraction.
- Lavender and sandalwood are good for relaxing and encouraging you to go with the flow.
- Lemon and rosemary are good for clarity, intelligence and general power.
- Ground cloves pack a magical punch and attract attention. Cloves have particularly strong drawing properties.
- Ginger is used for control and to bring about change. It is a fiery spice and can bring dramatic results, so use sparingly.
- Vanilla extract inspires love and romance and also has a pleasant aroma.

Think about the kind of scents you like, after all you may end up wearing this oil, so you want it to smell nice.

Many oils have astrological associations and you may want to choose scents that match your star sign. Perhaps there is a particular goddess you admire; if so, see if she has a particular scent or herb that can be used in your power oil. Hecate, Queen of the Witches, is often associated with cypress. So, if I wanted to incorporate her particular powers into my oil, I might use cypress essential oil as one of the ingredients.

Once you have decided on your ingredients, mix them together and decant. Remember to visualise as you prepare the oil. See yourself as a powerful goddess. See yourself achieving your heart's desires wearing this oil.

Make a note of the ingredients in your book of shadows, so that you can refer to it should you need to make up some more.

Keep the oil in a safe place. You might store it on your altar with other magical items, or surround it with crystals and gem stones to keep it charged with power.

3. Personal magnetism

This spell uses your personal power oil to enhance your personal magnetism.

Ingredients: Purple candle, power oil, sugar
Best day: The day of the week that you were born
Moon phase: Waxing

The day you were born is significant to you. Each day is associated with certain properties and planets, so it stands to reason that this will imbue you with power.

Dress the purple candle with your power oil. (Purple is the colour most associated with power and psychic development.) As you rub the oil into the candle, imagine your popularity and powers of attraction growing. Sprinkle a circle of sugar around the candle. Sugar has strong drawing properties. Now light the candle and watch it burn.

4. Cup of courage

There are times in life when we all need a cup of courage. Times when we need to steel and calm ourselves for some big event (even if it's only the arrival of the mother in law!). This tea will help to bolster and prepare you for such times.

Ingredients: Mint leaves, chamomile, honey
Best day: Any day you need a little extra courage
Moon phase: Best during a waxing Moon, but can be done any time

Steep the chamomile and mint in hot water, strain, and add honey to taste. The mint leaves help replenish a weary heart, the chamomile promotes courage and a calm mind and the honey is warm and nurturing. This combination cannot fail to prepare you for almost anything!

Spells for psychic development ⭐✦

There are many different ways to enhance your psychic abilities. The suggestions below are not so much spells as magical hints and tips that will help you to tap into your sixth sense.

Quartz crystal and amethyst

Wearing quartz crystal is said to open the channels for psychic communication. Amethyst is another stone associated with the third eye, the spot in the middle of your forehead which is used for psychic work. To activate your third eye, hold an amethyst on this spot and visualise a purple flower in the middle of your forehead. See the petals of the flower opening up. When you wish to close down from psychic work, do the same exercise, this time imagining that the petals of the flower are closing inwards. You can also sleep with an amethyst beneath your pillow; this is said to stimulate prophetic dreams.

Coffee

The aroma of fresh coffee brewing is said to promote psychic ability as well as reviving a depleted aura. You don't need to drink the coffee, just breathe in the aroma and relax.

Lavender

Lavender is another flower that is said to promote psychic ability. The scent of lavender relaxes the brain and makes it easier to communicate with the subconscious mind. Dab some lavender essential oil on your temples and also the third eye before meditation or psychic work. Rinse your hands in lavender water before using tarot cards.

Pine and pine cones

Fresh pine is a scent that stimulates the psychic muscles. Pine groves are often considered sacred and have been used by many cultures as locations for outdoor ritual. Keep a pine cone in your pocket to help you connect with your sixth sense. You can also use pine cones in charm bags for psychic development. For example, place a pine cone and a crystal in a purple or black pouch; add a couple of drops of lavender oil, or the flowers if you have easy access to them. Spit in the bag to seal the spell, and say:

I open up my mind, my third eye.
Let thoughts, feelings and impressions fly.
So mote it be.

You can also use pine oil in your bath, and let the scent transport you into the world of your subconscious. Try burning pine oil during visualisations to receive psychic messages.

The Moon

The Moon affects us in many ways. It affects our emotions, and our intuition. The night of the full Moon is a good time to receive psychic messages and premonitions. At full Moon, place a bowl of spring water outside under the Moon's rays. In the morning, take the water in, pour it into a bottle and keep it in a cool, dark place. Whenever you need psychic inspiration, rinse your hands and face in the water, paying special attention to the area of your third eye.

Chamomile tea

Chamomile tea is said to replenish the spirit as well as promote psychic development. Add a dollop of honey for taste and let the herbal benefits of the tea soothe you after any visualisations or psychic work.

Marigolds

There are many flowers and herbs said to encourage psychic skills, and marigolds are supposed to be incredibly potent in this area. You can put them in sleep pillows to induce prophetic dreams or sprinkle the flowers beneath your bed. The strength, vibrancy and scent of the flowers work to stimulate your psychic muscles.

Lettuce

Lettuce is a great natural sleep tonic. Eat lettuce leaves at night to encourage a peaceful night's sleep and prophetic dreams. It is also claimed that if you rub the leaves on your forehead, on the area of the third eye, this will bring insight. Try it before visualisation.

Celery

A little like lettuce, celery can be eaten to induce a deep sleep filled with meaningful dreams. The seeds in particular are said to stimulate psychic powers, and many witches use them in potions or burn them and inhale the scent before any psychic work. I suggest a simple salad of lettuce and celery before visualisation to cleanse the palate, clear the mind and help with relaxation.

Spells for protecting you and your home

As your powers grow as you dabble in psychic work, your aura will become more sensitive to the thoughts and feelings of those around you. You may want to shut this down at times, to distance yourself from the effects of others. There are many simple techniques that can be used (including the psychic egg mentioned in Chapter 2). There are also hundreds of spells that use ingredients to aid in protection. I have included a few here, and they can be used in conjunction with the visualisation techniques.

Spell-casting tips

Colours

The colour most associated with protection is black. Wearing black acts like a shield and will tone down an over-bright aura. Brown has earthy, grounding properties. Red is good for overcoming problems and asserting yourself. Blue is linked with healing. All of these colours can be used in protection spells.

Crystals

These can be placed around the home (one in every room on a window ledge) to protect the house and those that live within it.

Aloe vera

This plant has many healing and protective benefits. Keep an aloe vera plant on your altar/coffee table to lighten the atmosphere and protect you from unwanted influences.

Salt

Salt has long been known for its powers of protection. Sprinkle salt on your doorstep and around your property to keep intruders out. You can also bathe in sea salt when you feel in need of replenishment and protection.

Brick dust

Brick dust is often used in spells when you need to overcome someone or something. It has strong protective powers. Only a little is required and you can use it to protect your home by sprinkling some powder on your doorstep.

Eggs

These are wonderful tools for absorbing negativity. If you feel threatened and low, roll an egg over your body. Imagine the egg is drawing out all of the badness in your aura. When you have finished, smash the egg and take the remains out of your house. If you can, bury the egg in the soil so that the negative influences can be absorbed and transformed.

Garlic

This is an obvious choice here, but it doesn't just repel vampires! It has long been believed that garlic protects from all sorts of evils. Make a simple wreath of garlic and place it over your front door. I wouldn't suggest leaving it there too long – if nothing else, the smell of rotting garlic will put off unwanted *and* wanted visitors!

Angels

Do you believe in angels? Well, there's nothing more reassuring than knowing that your guardian angel is watching over and protecting you. A simple prayer to your angel asking for help and protection can have amazing results.

Iron

A hard and rigid metal, iron is a strong antidote to evil; it acts as a repellent, and can be used when you feel under psychic attack. The best way to use iron for protection is to keep a piece about your person, or wear some as jewellery. Make an amulet out of a piece of iron, or place an iron nail in a drawstring pouch with a crystal and some salt as a protection charm.

Climbing plants

Honeysuckle is said to have protective qualities. Grow it in abundance in your garden if you can. Similarly, ivy growing upon the house is said to protect it from evil influences.

1. Simple candle protection spell

Ingredients: Black candle, aloe vera oil, salt

Best day: Any, but Monday in particular, as you can call on the influence of the Moon and the goddess Hecate. Hecate protects and nurtures witches and helps with the development of psychic powers. If you feel under threat spiritually, or susceptible to the evil around you, call on her to help protect you and your surroundings.

Moon phase: Again, any, although protection spells work very well during the waning Moon, and if you are going to call upon Hecate, it's wise to do this during the dark of the Moon – the last three days of the lunar cycle.

Take the black candle (you might be able to get candles in the shape of witches or black cats, which are excellent for protection spells) and anoint it with aloe vera oil. While you are doing this, visualise yourself and your home protected from negative influences and people. Sprinkle a circle of salt around the candle and light it.

If you are contacting Hecate, say a few words to request her assistance and to thank her for watching over you and yours. Let the candle burn out naturally.

2. Blueberry and sage protection infusion

Blueberries are not only incredibly healthy but also have magical protective qualities. This spell can be adapted to protect you physically and also to protect your home.

Ingredients: Blueberry leaves, sage leaves
Best day: Any
Moon phase: Waning, or whenever you need extra protection

Take a small bowl of blueberry leaves and sage and pour boiling water on them to infuse. Leave for five minutes and strain the liquid into a cup. Drink while visualising health and protection.

You can also use this infusion around the house to cleanse and protect the environment and those who live there. Waft the aroma from the warm liquid in every room of your house.

3. Symbol spell

There are many magical symbols for protection; most of them can be traced back to the female genitalia. This part of a woman is said to be sacred and highly powerful, and as such over the centuries and in folklore, various symbols which allude to this part of the anatomy have been used in magical protection spells. The following spell uses an upside-down triangle, which is said to reflect the female genitalia.

Ingredients: Red brick dust, paper
Best day: Any
Moon phase: Any

Collect some red brick dust, and on a piece of paper arrange the dust in an upside-down triangle. Leave the paper near your front door to ward off unwanted visitors. If you can't find red brick dust, red or black ink works just as well. For added protection and security, you can also draw the triangles on the walls of your house before you decorate.

4. Protection charm bag

Ingredients: Lavender, patchouli oil, salt, red drawstring bag
Best day: Any
Moon phase: Any

Take a sprig of lavender and place it a red bag or pouch, add a couple of drops of patchouli oil and a pinch of salt and then spit in the bag to seal the spell (it adds the extra protective strength of your saliva to the mix).

Keep this charm bag about your person at all times for constant protection.

 # 5. Personal protection juice

There are times when we might feel under attack. Perhaps we're not feeling so good physically and this affects our emotional well-being. This is a very simple juice that gives a magical boost and helps with feelings of protection and self-preservation.

Ingredients: Mango, blueberries, cranberries, lemon juice, ice
Best day: Any
Moon phase: Any

Blend together the peeled mango, blueberries, cranberries, and a handful of ice. When the drink is ready, add some freshly squeezed lemon juice. Lemon is good for purification and cleansing as well as promoting love, and in this case self-love.

CHAPTER TWELVE

Spells on the move

Magical workings may have been around since the beginning of time, but that doesn't mean they don't move with the times! Modern magic is sassy and can be adapted to every situation. It's part of the urban big picture and can be used on the streets, in the office, virtually anywhere that you are, because in essence the magic comes from you. Of course, you couldn't whip up an altar and start performing candle magic in the middle of the office; neither could you burn oils and herbs while commuting to work. You have to consider the constraints you have and be flexible. But that's a beauty of magic, it *is* flexible. It's a fluid medium that can be changed to suit your needs.

This chapter is all about magic you can do on the move. Magic you take with you, without having to carry any magical tools (other than those you have at your fingertips or in your handbag). These are simple spells and magical techniques that will enliven your world. You will notice that most of the techniques described involve a level of visualisation, because the power of your mind is available to you any time. Nobody knows what goes on in our heads as we go about our daily business, and it's just as well – we wouldn't want our innermost thoughts available for general consumption. On the other hand, this is the secret key to mobile magic: you have the greatest magical tool in your head. It's your imagination and the ability to use it anywhere.

Handbag magic

Handbag magic is about using what you have available at the time. As you become more adept at spells, you will realise that you don't need hundreds of ingredients and long elaborate rituals to achieve results. Magic is primarily about tapping into the power within, and focusing your intention. If you can do this, you have the key to perform your magic anywhere. There are many spells that can be done on the move, and you can adapt any of those below, and create your own as you become more confident. Being able to visualise what you want is the first step. Some people find it hard to visualise anything while they go about their business, and it does take practice to focus the mind. Try this simple visualisation at any point during your day. It will calm your mind, and relax you and also helps with picturing things in busy environments.

Relax and free your mind

Picture yourself standing on an isolated beach. The sea is lapping at the shore and you can see for miles all around. For a moment, just focus on that, on the feel of the breeze upon your cheek, on the smell of salt in the air. Try to feel the sand beneath your feet.

Now explore. This is your beach and you can go anywhere and do anything. You may want to paddle in the sea, you may want to sit and play with the sand in your fingers. You may want to walk along the

★ beach and see where it leads. Give yourself free rein on this. You may ★

★ encounter other people. Let these things happen and enjoy them. ★

★ When you are ready, take a deep breath and return to your world ★

★ as it is, feeling calm, refreshed and as if you've just had a mini break ★

★ somewhere hot and sunny! ★

✪ 1. Beauty booster

Ingredients: Any make-up you have in your handbag
Best day: Any
Moon phase: Any

I'm starting with a simple magical technique that could be considered cheating! You might want to perform this before you take to the streets. However, it's also something you could do anywhere. Take your main beauty products (perhaps lipstick, mascara, powder) and hold them in your hands. Direct your will into the products and imagine a stream of light passing from the middle of your forehead (your third eye) into each product. The light fills each product with magical qualities so that every time you apply it, you sparkle and your aura shines that little bit brighter. You can choose to say a few words quietly as you do this. Something like:

With this light I make you shine,
And in turn you brighten all that is mine.
So mote it be.

✪ 2. Magical Mirror

Ingredients: Make-up compact mirror
Best day: Any, although this works especially well on Mondays
Moon phase: Any

The magical mirror is an essential part of any witch's tool kit; but it doesn't have to be a special, ornate hand-held mirror – a simple make-up compact does the trick. Some witches like to leave their mirror out on the night of a full Moon to charge it, but this is not essential. You can charge it by a simple visualisation using white light.

Imagine that a pure white light is passing down through the crown of your head as you breathe. This is the universal cleansing light. As you breathe out, picture yourself breathing the light into the mirror and charging it with power.

Now, whenever you need a boost, at any time during your day, you can take out your special mirror and gaze into it. Imagine as you do so that the universal light is reflected back in your features, lifting and brightening your aura and making you feel altogether wonderful and sexy! This spell is so easy, you can even do it on public transport, all it requires is a little belief and the ability to visualise.

3. Protection on the move

There are many times in our daily life when we might feel vulnerable. Sometimes for obvious reasons, such as someone persecuting us or being followed, and sometimes we can't explain the feelings. Here are a couple of visualisation techniques that you can use in any type of situation where you feel as though you need extra protection.

Ingredients: Just yourself
Best day: Any
Moon phase: Any

The first visualisation involves imagining you are in a golden suit of armour, almost like a space suit. The material is flexible and covers your clothes and also acts as a form of psychic protection. Wherever you are, imagine that you are in your golden suit of armour. A little like the psychic egg, this field of energy sits around you like a shell so that any negative feelings that come your way bounce from the armour straight back to where they came from.

The second technique can be used either on its own or to reinforce the golden suit of armour, or the psychic egg. In the area just above your navel and below the breastbone (the solar plexus) visualise a pentagram. (The pentagram is the witches' symbol of protection and very potent.) In your mind's eye, see it glowing white as if etched into your skin. If you are employing the psychic egg method, see the pentagram etched into the golden shell that surrounds you; imagine it like a badge of honour adding extra strength to your aura. You can also do this with the suit of armour, or even visualise the pentagram as a symbol on your shield.

4. Projecting the future!

Do you have an important event that you need to go well? Perhaps there's a tricky meeting ahead, or you have to give a presentation and want to make the right impression. This quick spell will help.

Ingredients: Your mind
Best day: Any day when you have an important event
Moon phase: Any

To add extra oomph to this spell, you might want to carry some personal power oil with you and anoint your temples and neck with it, just like applying perfume. In the moments leading up to the event, or as you are travelling to or preparing for it, see yourself there, doing it – at the meeting, giving the presentation. See your aura shining brightly. See everything you do as a huge success. See the people impressed with your work.

Now take one picture from this slide show in your mind, a picture that sums up the outcome you would like. Put the picture in a frame of white light. Imagine it is like a bubble of light, with your outcome sealed inside.

The next stage is to set the image free as if you are releasing a balloon. See the image sail off into the distance and as it goes, say a few words in your head; something like:

As I have seen, so mote it be!

The future may not be exactly as you had pictured it, but by doing this exercise you are promoting feelings of confidence in the outcome. You are setting in motion a trail of events to suit your needs.

5. Invisibility spell

We all have times when we would like to be invisible. Sometimes it's to avoid major disasters or confrontations, and other times it's simply because we don't feel like talking to someone in the supermarket, or we're trying to avoid an over-zealous ex! We could just be having an 'off' day. Try this simple technique; it's amazing how often it works.

Ingredients: Nothing! (Well you are trying to be invisible after all!)
Best day: Any day when you need to fade into the background
Moon phase: Any, although a waning Moon might help

Visualise a black cloak around you; it cloaks you from head to foot in invisibility. You move quietly, gliding past unnoticed. The cloak darkens down the brightness of your aura. As you are wearing the cloak, go about your daily business as normal, there is no need to sneak about. The visualisation is enough to help you go unnoticed in tricky situations. In fact, the more you try to hide the more conspicuous you will appear, as you are focusing on not being noticed, which has the opposite effect!

✦ 6. *Car parking angel*

There are angels for everything and you can enlist their help whenever you like. The car parking angel is always at hand and very accommodating.

Ingredients: An open mind!
Best day: Whenever you need to find a car parking space
Moon phase: Any

All you have to do is, before you begin your journey, say a short prayer asking the angel for help when you reach your destination to find the perfect car parking space. You can also do this as you travel, as long as it doesn't distract you too much from the road!

✦ 7. *Finding lost objects*

Ingredients: A honed intention to find what you seek!
Best day: The day you lose something
Moon phase: Any

Again this requires a little faith and self belief, but it's amazing how many times it actually works. If you are out and about and you lose something (this happens to me a lot!), rather than panic, take a moment, take a breath and ask the universe to assist you. Say a simple spell in your mind:

> *What has gone is found.*
> *What I seek is all round.*
> *Help me see it clear.*
> *Bring my lost [item] here!*
> *So mote it be*

It may seem far-fetched, but it's incredible the number of times this brings results. It works on many levels: asking the universe for help, clearing your mind and focusing your intention, and reducing any worry which might blind you to finding the item. More often than not it's misplaced in front of your eyes, but panic can make us oblivious to the obvious at times.

Wishing spells

Wishing spells can be carried out anywhere, although it usually helps if you tie the spell to a day that has particular significance, such as love wishes on a Friday, business success on a Thursday, wishes for creativity on a Wednesday. It also helps if you consider the phase of the Moon. A full Moon is the perfect time to make any kind of wish. A new Moon is also good for the start of projects, and any time when the Moon is waxing is favourable.

A wishing spell is just what it says on the label: you make a wish, focus on your intention, hold a specific image in your mind's eye, and then let it go. Always remember to release your wish because the tighter you try to hold onto something, the more it eludes you.

There are more elaborate wishing spells which use the four compass directions and offerings of herbs and spices with various chants, but at the end of the day it's *your* wish, your personal magic, and you can create the spell to suit your needs and limitations.

If you feel you want to do something to seal your spell, you could try the following, as long as you are not in polite company! You could spit to affirm your spell, or use your saliva by wetting your index finger and drawing a pentagram in the air to seal and protect your magical intentions.

The fun thing about magic on the move is that it is spontaneous and creative. It allows you to tap into your imagination and trust your intuition, which has to be a good thing. The more you trust your senses, the more successful you will become in every area of your life.

Cyber magic

Magic does have a place in this high-tech computerised world. It can help to keep us healthy and motivated, it can help us to deal with frustrations and technical difficulties, and it can help when all else fails. Experiment and see!

1. Amethyst inspiration spell

Everyone knows that working continuously at a computer can have a detrimental effect on your health. Being hunched over a work station can affect posture, causing shoulder, neck and back pain, and, depending on how long you stare at the computer screen, impair your vision and cause headaches and dizzy spells. Most companies encourage regular five-minute breaks to combat negative effects, but what about the detrimental effects on your spiritual health?

There is nothing more tiring than staring at a blank computer screen. I have spoken to many office workers who claim that it's almost as if the computer sucks the creative life-force from them. Dramatic as this may sound, many people believe that computers have a draining effect on auras, and this in turn can affect energy levels and creativity. To help prevent this and if you're in need of a little creative input, invest in a piece of amethyst. Keep it on your desk near your computer screen. You can charge the amethyst with positive energy and every time you need a little pick me up or some inspiration, take the stone in your hands, place it on your third eye (in the middle of your forehead) and feel its magical influences seeping into your conscious mind. Regularly cleanse the stone in salt water to get rid of any negative energies it has absorbed.

2. Healing hands

It may sound completely daft to suggest that you can heal your computer by laying your hands upon the hard drive, and it *would* be ridiculous to do this without trying the usual methods of fixing problems first. However, for those of us desperate enough (and those who have tried every other method and are just about ready to hit it with a hammer), then perhaps a little magic might work. There have been incidences in the past where the energy of a person's aura has sent electrical equipment slightly haywire. It is often suggested that people with highly developed psychic skills can have a strange effect on electrical items about the house. If this is the case, surely it might also work the other way round? The next time your computer plays up at home or work (and if you don't mind some odd looks from your colleagues) take a moment to perform this healing technique.

Wait until you are ready to leave for the day, so that you are giving the healing time to work its magic over night. Place your hands on the hard drive of your computer and take a deep breath. Imagine pure white healing light travelling down through the top of your head, down through your shoulders and arms until it reaches your hands. Now see this energy pouring from your hands into the computer. See the energy absorbed into the workings of the hard drive and feel things shifting, working, slotting into place. This may only take a few minutes. Now shut down your computer so it can rest. You never know, when you restart it in the morning you may have a pleasant surprise!

3. 'Phone me' spell

If there really were a way to make someone call you when you wanted them to, women all over the world would have been using it for centuries! As it is, we hope and pray and stare longingly at the phone in the hope that this will make it ring. However, there are times in our lives, including our working lives, when we really need someone to get in touch with us. It's amazing how this works when the need *isn't*

there. Most people have at some time or other thought about a person and at that instant the phone rings and the person is on the other end of the line. Coincidence, quite possibly, but if we could turn this sequence of events around, and on occasion make that psychic connection work for us, we would save a fortune in text messages!

This technique relies on relaxed effort. Those two words appear to contradict each other, but you need to have a clear picture in your mind of what you want. So, in the case of getting someone to call, you have to be able to picture them in your head, see them picking up the phone to call you, hear your phone ringing, hear the caller's voice at the other end. See and hear all these things in clear detail. See it as a film of events in your mind, then freeze-frame on the last image and as you do so place it in a bubble and watch it drift away into the distance.

The key to obtaining anything is to see yourself with it, and then let it go. Let go of your desire for it and trust that it will come to you. It's very difficult to let go when you want something badly, but learning to trust in your magical abilities helps. If you can perfect this technique (and it does take time and lots of practice), you will see some amazing results.

CHAPTER THIRTEEN

Spells for sleeping and dreaming

Dreaming is something we all do. It's not something that happens *to* us; it's something we can control and use to our advantage. Dreaming is a way of clearing away the clutter that we collect in our heads every day, so, in effect, it's essential for our general well-being. Everyone dreams and most of us every night, although we don't always remember our dreams. Some might say that's a good thing. Dreams can be wonderful and weird, but sometimes upsetting and frightening. It's certainly no fun when you suffer from recurring nightmares, but even the scariest of dreams has a point.

Dreams open up new vistas; they act as a portal to our inner world, our hopes and fears. In dreams, we receive guidance, answers to questions. We can see solutions to problems that occur in our waking life. Dreams are a place where we can encounter spirit guides and angels and learn to communicate with them. It's amazing to think about everything that goes on when we sleep, that we can enter this fabulous new world and learn so much.

Of course, to do this effectively you need to cultivate an open and relaxed mind. You need to be able to recall your dreams and interpret them. Much of this will happen naturally as you continue with your magical work, but there are many things you can do to help the process.

In a way, visualisation is a form of daydreaming, which is also something essential to our emotional and spiritual health. When we daydream, we imagine things as we would like them to be, however far-fetched. We picture our wildest dreams and desires, we see and feel them, and although some might say we're away with the fairies, we are actually very much in control of our dream-like state. It's possible to carry this effect over into our sleeping mind and learn to control our dreams. This kind of dream manipulation is called lucid dreaming, and it can be a wonderful tool when you are trying to make sense of things happening in your life, or you are looking for specific answers.

This chapter includes spells to help with sleep, and some specifically to encourage dreams. There are spells to help with dream prophecy and understanding the images and messages in your dreams. There are also hints and tips for communicating with spirit guides in your dreams.

The most important thing to remember when working with dreams is that you are safe and secure in your dream landscape. This is a world that you create and even nightmares can teach us something if we look beyond the initial shock.

Tips for a good night's sleep

Naturally, if you want to work with dreams, the first thing you need to be able to do is sleep! A busy life with many stresses can often hinder sleep patterns and leave you feeling tired and depressed. A good night's sleep is restorative and energising and therefore very important to put you in the right frame of mind to face the day (and for any magical work). Here are a few tips, magical and otherwise to help you drift off.

Lavender oil

Lavender has soothing, relaxing properties. Leave bunches around the house to infuse your home with harmony. Pour a couple of drops of the essential oil in your bath at night, or dab the oil upon your temples and just above your brow in the centre of your forehead: the third eye. Massage this spot with your finger in circular movements and visualise yourself falling into a deep sleep. Then see your third eye opening, see it as a purple flower whose petals are slowly stretching outwards to reveal a spiralling centre of light. This will encourage the flow of dreams.

Milk and honey

Not so much a magical remedy, but definitely a soothing sleep-inducing drink. Heat up some milk to room temperature, and stir in a spoonful of honey. Milk has calming, nurturing properties and the honey is sweet and satisfying and will help to ease away worries. Drink this about half an hour before going to bed.

Alternatively, a sprinkle of nutmeg in warm milk can have a similar soothing effect as well as a pleasant taste. Incidentally the mix of hot milk and honey can also be used in a magical bath to induce sleep. You can add some drops of Lavender and Rosemary essential oil to make the potion more powerful, and add to a warm bath before going to bed.

Lettuce tea

This might sound an unlikely brew, but lettuce is renowned for its ability to promote sleep. Steep some lettuce leaves in boiling water.

Drain and serve as a tea. You can sweeten this with honey if preferred.

Salad supper

As above, lettuce leaves can help promote sleep, and so can celery seeds, so the next time you get the urge for a late-night nibble, why not make up a salad with lettuce and celery. These foods are easy to digest and will encourage a restful sleep.

Remember, as with any of these suggestions, visualise!

Yarrow

Yarrow is a plant that grows with small white and sometimes lilac flowers. It has many medicinal and magical uses, and can be used to soothe digestion and as a very mild sedative. You may have yarrow growing in your garden, as it is a common weed. If so, make an infusion to drink as a tea. If not, many herbal and health shops have various forms of yarrow teas or tinctures which can help with insomnia.

Hormonal help

Periods of insomnia are often caused by a hormonal imbalance. If you think this may be the case, try the following. Make an infusion of nettle leaves to drink (you can also buy nettle tea ready made from most health food shops). Also invest in lemon balm essential oil and add a couple of drops to your bath before bedtime, or burn the oil to fill your home with its calm and refreshing aroma. This will help to balance your hormones.

To encourage a peaceful sleep

Ingredients: Cardamom pods (a handful), salt, sage leaves, lavender essential oil
Best day: At night, any that you want a good night's sleep
Moon phase: Any

This spell involves making a pillow to either hang above your bed or place beneath your usual sleeping pillow. You can use a drawstring pouch if you don't fancy sewing squares of material together. Grind the cardamom pods and the salt with the sage leaves, then place the mixture in the pouch or pillow. Add three drops of lavender essential oil. Spit to seal the spell. While grinding the mixture, remember to visualise a peaceful night's sleep.

Spells to encourage dreams

The first thing to ask yourself is what kind of dreams do you want? Do you want solutions to problems? Answers to questions? Are you looking to dream of the future, and, if so, what particular area of your life would you like to know about? Perhaps you want to dream of someone who has passed away? Or maybe you would like to use dream-time to connect with your spirit guide or angel? There are many different types of dreams and ways you can use them. It may be that you want to *prevent* certain dreams, keep nightmares at bay; there are spells to help with this too. So, before you prepare your spell, think about what it is you really want. Make sure you have your intention clear in your head.

Have fun with your dreams. They are a part of you; they unlock the secrets of the future and the mysteries of the past. Working with dreams encourages the flow of magic in both your sleeping and waking world. Sweet dreams!

1. To help you remember your dreams

It's all very well deciding that you want to work with your dreams, but before you do anything you need to ensure that you will actually remember what it is you dream about. Most nights we have several dreams, but remember only a few, if any (usually the last one is the most potent). Here is a simple but effective technique to recall your dreams. It relies on a little belief in mind over matter, as does most magic!

Make a cup of your favourite night time beverage – chamomile tea works well, as does hot milk, honey and nutmeg. Take this to bed with you. As you drink your tea, visualise yourself sleeping soundly, then say the following affirmation:

Tonight I will dream, and on waking I will remember my dreams.

Finish your drink and settle down to sleep. It's as easy as that! The statement is affirmed in your mind as you begin to relax and enter the world of sleep. This is the last thing your conscious mind will recall, and this statement will seep into your subconscious and help you to remember your dreams on waking.

This technique can also be used with Moon water. Charge a bottle of spring water in the light of a full Moon (leave it outside all night in your garden). Keep it refrigerated and when you need to recall your dreams, take a glass of the charged water to bed with you. Have a sip before you go to sleep and a sip on waking before recording your dreams in a notebook.

✸ 2. To dream about a lost loved one

Ingredients: Photograph of your loved one, white candle, lavender oil, quartz crystal or piece of amethyst

Best day: Any day, but Mondays are particularly good as they are ruled by the Moon and this can assist with psychic skills and uncovering the veils between worlds. Also consider trying this technique on Halloween night, the time when the spirits of those departed are said to return.

Moon phase: Any

On the evening that you wish to dream about your lost loved one, light a white candle, anointed with lavender oil if you wish. Hold a picture of your loved one in your hands. Remember all the wonderful things about this person. Let memories of the times you have shared run through your mind. Place the photograph in front of the candle, then take the crystal or amethyst. Hold it in your hands and say the following:

> *Across the boundaries of time and space I call to you.*
> *I hold the memory of your face, I talk to you.*
> *On this night within my dreams you come to me.*
> *In heart and mind, so mote it be.*

When you go to bed, place the photograph and the crystal beneath your pillow. Next dab a couple of drops of lavender oil on your third eye. Continue to do this for the next three nights to help encourage dreams and communication with your departed loved one.

This spell is very effective. Remember to keep a dream journal and note down any dreams that you can recall while doing this. Sometimes our lost loved ones will communicate with us in pictures and symbols, so pay particular attention to images in your dreams at this time. The meanings may not be obvious at first, but a few days later it may all become clear. Often loved ones communicate with us in our dreams and give us special messages for the future, so it's important to write everything down, however insignificant it seems to be at the time.

3. Dream oil for prophetic dreams

Dream oils can be applied directly to the body before bedtime. They are ideal for a relaxing pre-sleep massage, or you can use them as a body lotion. Almond oil is the ideal base, but you can use sunflower and/or olive oil if needs be.

Gardenia essential oil is quite difficult to get hold of. Many oils claim to be gardenia, but are just a reproduction of the scent, so it is well worth getting hold of the real thing if you want to encourage prophetic dreams. Gardenias have strong magical properties; they aid psychic development and promote powerful dreams.

Ingredients: Gardenia flowers and/or essential oil, lavender essential oil, almond oil
Best day: Any
Moon phase: Any

Take a cup of almond oil and add a couple of drops of lavender oil and gardenia oil. If you can get hold of the fresh flowers too, then make an infusion with hot water and bathe in it. This will also have the same effect as the oil.

Once you have created your dream oil, massage it into your skin before sleeping.

You can experiment with dream oils adding different scents to suit. Other essential oils that can be used to encourage happy dreams include rose, pettigrain, orange, ylang ylang, frankincense and myrrh. The more oils you use the less amount of each you need to include. So if you're using two or more, just a couple of drops each will be sufficient.

✪ 4. Tea for prophetic dreams

Ingredients: Rose petals, honey
Best day: Any
Moon phase: Any

Fresh rose petals make excellent prophetic teas. Wash the petals and infuse them in hot water and add a spoonful of honey to taste. Drink before bedtime. You can encourage different types of dreams by choosing different coloured petals. So, if you're looking for some passion in your dream encounters, use red petals; pink petals encourage romantic dreams; white petals are excellent for healing and psychic messages; and yellow petals will promote happy and relaxing dreams.

5. Psychic dream pillow

Mugwort encourages dreaming and also helps you to remember dreams. Lavender relaxes the mind and is known to encourage sleep.

Ingredients: Piece of muslin or a handkerchief, dried mugwort, dried lavender
Best day: Any
Moon phase: Any

A small piece of muslin or soft fabric can be used to make a little pillow. If you're not a keen sewer, you can tie the contents up in a handkerchief using thread or ribbon. Fill the pillow with mugwort and lavender and place it beneath your pillow at night.

Warning: Mugwort should not be used by pregnant women or those trying to get pregnant as it's known to stimulate menstruation.

6. Tarot spell for divination

The tarot, with its beautiful images and symbols can be used in magic spells, in particular the Major Arcana (the picture cards as opposed to the cards split into suits). The Major Arcana tells the story of the Fool's journey, and the symbols in these cards are powerful. You don't need to know the meanings of the cards to be able to get an impression. Invest in a tarot pack and take your time looking through the cards. Ask yourself how each card makes you feel. What kind of emotions do the images conjure?

The Moon is a card of illusion, a card that rules the unseen in our world. Sometimes it's a card of delusion, it signifies the things we know but deny because we don't want to see the truth. The Moon rules our subconscious, the part of our mind that comes to the fore when we dream. It also rules our creativity.

Spend some time looking at the image of the Moon, and thinking about it what it means to you. When you go to bed place the card beneath your pillow. Give thanks to the Moon and ask for her special powers to illuminate your sleeping mind and present you with prophetic dreams. Ask the Moon to help you connect with your spirit guide. Remember to note down any impressions you have on waking.

✪ 7. To see a future lover

Ingredients: Piece of rose quartz, handkerchief or tissue, rose water, three apple seeds

Best day: Friday night

Moon phase: Waxing; this spell is particularly potent on the night of a full Moon.

Cut open an apple and remove three of the seeds. As you do this, say:

Apple of love, bring to me a vision of eternity.
Bring me the face of my future love
In dreams that are blessed from up above.
So mote it be.

Next take the handkerchief and sprinkle a couple of drops of rose water on it. Wrap the seeds up in the handkerchief and place this under your pillow with a piece of rose quartz. When you go to bed you can repeat the chant one more time. Happy dreaming!

✪ 8. For erotic dreams

Fancy a bit of action in your dreams? Perhaps you want a dream lover? Then this is the spell for you and it's so simple. It uses catnip, which is not just loved by cats; it's a wonderful herb that can be used in love and sex spells.

Ingredients: Catnip, cloves, red rose petals (fresh or dried)
Best day: Any, but Friday nights work particularly well
Moon phase: Waxing, ideally

Take a box or a jar and fill it with some catnip and a handful of cloves and rose petals. Keep it closed on your bedside table until you are ready for bed, then open and it and breathe in the aroma while asking for an erotic encounter in your dreams.

 ## 9. Dream travel

It's possible to travel to all manner of exotic locations in your dreams. This is called astral travel, and it involves you being in control of your dream self and directing the dream, almost like directing a film. You can implant ideas into your subconscious before you go to sleep to help with this. The key to successful lucid dreaming is being able to relax and trust your subconscious. Visualisation also helps: the more you are able to picture things clearly in your mind's eye, the more trained your subconscious becomes. Try the following exercise as you lie in bed.

Get hold of a picture or a scene that you really like. Choose something you love looking at and that inspires good feelings, as you will be working very closely with it. You might even pick a particular tarot card image. Focus on the picture, taking in every detail.

Now close your eyes and recall the picture to your mind. Try to remember everything as clearly as possible. Now imagine that you are stepping into the picture. See yourself step over the edge into this new world of colour and texture. Look around you, marvel at how wonderful everything looks. Explore and have fun with this. Think of somewhere that you would love to go. It can be somewhere that you've been before or somewhere completely new. As long as you can picture it, that's all that matters. Once you have the image clear in your mind, try stepping into it, and let your mind drift.

This technique can lead to some wonderful dreams, and because you implanted the idea with your conscious mind before sleep you will find that you are still able to exercise some control over your dreams.

Tips to prevent nightmares

There are many different ways to prevent bad dreams. Here are just a few magical suggestions.

Rosemary

The herb rosemary has long been known for its protective powers. Take a sprig and soak it in warm salt water. Remove the Rosemary and sprinkle a few drops of the anointed water in each corner of your bedroom. This keeps negativity at bay. You can also hang the Rosemary above your head, or place it beneath your pillow when you have finished.

Protective pot pourri

You can make up your own scented pot pourri to leave on your bedside table. This will help to dispel bad dreams and encourage a restful night's sleep. The following herbs and scents are useful:

• Sage
• Rosemary
• Parsley
• Cinnamon
• Nutmeg
• Cloves
• Lemon
• Juniper

• Wormwood (not easily accessible but can be ordered from specialist shops on the internet).

Alternatively, take a small jar and fill it with a mixture of these herbs. Seal the lid tightly and keep it by your bed. Before going to sleep, open the jar and inhale the aroma, visualising yourself having a peaceful night's sleep.

The witch's symbol

I have mentioned the pentagram in previous chapters, particularly on psychic defence. It's the symbol most associated with witchcraft, and has strong protective qualities. If you are plagued by nightmares, try this ritual.

Ingredients: Black candle, paper and pen
Best day: Any day
Moon phase: Any, although spells of protection work particularly well during a waning Moon

Light the candle. Imagine you are surrounded by protective white light. Feel the warm, uplifting energy of that light fill you up inside; feel strength oozing into your body, filling you with confidence. Next take a piece of paper and draw a pentagram on it. (If you have problems drawing a pentagram freehand, trace one before the spell and draw over it.) Then say the following words:

With this star I will stay strong,
Protected from this moment on.
Surrounded by a pure white light
That stays with me both day and night.

When you go to bed, place the picture of the symbol beneath your pillow to protect you while you sleep.

CHAPTER FOURTEEN

Magic and the environment

Remember that casting a spell is like cooking a fine meal. You prepare your ingredients, you put your heart and soul into the creation and cooking, and finally you sit down and enjoy the delicious results. Now we have reached that special part of the feast, the moment most of us look forward to – *the dessert*.

How do you draw your magic work to a close? The answer is you don't. Once you have opened the door to magic and accessed your witchy Inner Goddess, you have acknowledged the magic that is all around. You know it's there; you have experienced the power first hand. You will never be able to look at life in the same way. This is a good thing!

You have been given the secret formula to happiness. Everyday activities are still routine, but they will never be mundane, because you have the ability to see magic in everything. You can use the gifts you have been given to improve any situation, and the best part is that you don't have to stray from your daily schedule. Anything is possible, and everything is available. Now doesn't that leave a delightful taste in your mouth, and without those extra calories?

Healing yourself, the world and the washing machine ★ ★

Of course, there is always more you can do. Once you become aware of your inherent power you can use it to heal yourself, and your environment. Don't forget that magic can be applied to the rest of the world.

A magical way of life means that you appreciate the value of everything, and in particular the importance of nature. By working with plants and herbs, the seasons and planets, you attune yourself to the Earth, so make sure you look after it.

Here are some practical things you can do to nurture the Earth:
• Start a herb garden.
• Visit local parks and gardens; use them and look after them.
• Teach your children about nature.
• Join a society and work towards improving the environment.
• Go organic in every way possible.
• Grow your own vegetables and fruit.
• Recycle!

Create spells and simple rituals to celebrate the seasons. Make the most of the skills you have. It might only seem like one small wish for world peace, but every positive thought has an effect. Sometimes all it takes is a hug – don't underestimate the power of touch and kindness. It's magic in one of its many forms.

You can also use spells to heal things within the home. If the washing machine decides to pack up on a spin cycle, try a spell to remove blockages before you call out the plumber. It sounds far-fetched, but stranger things have happened!

When things go wrong (home appliances or situations), carry in your hand a set of keys (which are sacred to the goddess Hecate who removes obstacles) to a three-way crossroads. Ask Hecate to remove the blockage or barrier and make things run smoothly. Leave a clove of garlic as an offering to her.

Magical interiors

I'm not talking design here, although the simple layout of a room can have an effect on your life, as feng shui has shown. I'm talking about the little things you can do to each room in your house to make it more magical.

Take a look at your house, room by room, and think of the magical things you can do to enhance the activity that goes on in that room. Once you start, you will find there are countless things you can do to make the best of your home, and to keep those who live there happy and healthy.

Bathroom

The bathroom is a special room when you think about it: it's the place where you cleanse yourself every day, the place where you put on your face to the world and also the place where you can relax and let cares and stresses fall from your shoulders. Its physical purpose is clear, but its psychic purpose is equally as important.

Accessories

Think about it for a moment. We fill our bathrooms with various lotions and potions in the hope that they will make us feel and look better. So where is the harm in giving these things a little magical help? Keep a selection of useful oils handy on your bathroom shelf: lavender for relaxing, tea tree for antiseptic uses, ylang ylang for creating a romantic mood. All of these essential oils can be added to your bath while you visualise how you want to feel. Candles not only look attractive, but can be used in magical spells during bath time, so keep a selection around the room.

Colours

Consider the colours you use in your bathroom, not only for decoration but also for those added extras. Towels in particular are used to dry and rub away the debris we collect on a daily basis. Whilst doing this imagine that the towel is also rubbing away all the negative energy and stress that you have collected in your aura. Use white and blue towels to help absorb stress. Soaps too can be chosen because of their colour and scent.

Furnishings

The bathroom mirror shows your reflection, it shows how you look to others, the face you present to the world. Just as make-up mirrors can be used for magic, so can bigger mirrors around the house. Wipe the bathroom mirror with rose water and as you do so, say a few words to reinforce your image and make you feel beautiful and confident whenever you look into the mirror.

Finally the toilet – it might not seem like a magical implement, but it is. Think about the function it performs. It flushes things away. So it can be used in spells to flush things out of your life; things that you no longer need, or things that have a bad influence on you. If there is something that you would like rid of, write it down on a piece of paper, or on the shell of an egg. Go to the toilet and say a few words, something like:

I now release you from my life.

Away you go to end my strife.

Then drop the paper in the toilet bowl (if you have an egg, crack it and drop the contents in the bowl) and then flush.

Kitchen

The kitchen is the place where you prepare your magical meals. The place that helps you provide sustenance for yourself and your family. The kitchen can also be quite a social area, a place where you eat together and have conversations. The kitchen is a key room and can be the hub of the house, so it's quite a powerful place. Here are some ways to make it even more magical.

Accessories

Keep pots of fresh herbs on your window sill. It's good to have something growing in this part of the house, and herbs all have different properties. Sage is very good for cleansing an area of negativity, and basil encourages the flow of wealth and prosperity.

Fridge magnets are an excellent invention. Not only can they be used to brighten up your fridge and stick notes and reminders for all to see, they can also be used to create magic. Take a spell you have been developing that requires some time to work. Write it down. Write the words that you would say on special paper while visualising your aim and then stick it up on your fridge. Every time you go to your fridge door you'll see the spell and repeat it in your head. The rest of the family will also see it, and read it, therefore reinforcing the spell and your intentions.

Fridge poetry is another excellent and fun way to use spells creatively. Make up poems and spells and stick them on your fridge. Write affirmations of things you would like to manifest, and get everyone else to join in.

Tools

Charge your cooking implements before you use them, so that they bring out the nutrition of the food you are cooking. Charge your food (as mentioned before). You can charge it for any particular purpose and it really does make cooking an enjoyable experience.

Keep a brush or broom near your door and regularly sweep over your floor, imagining that you are sweeping away any negative influences. You can also use this activity to encourage movement in a particular area of your life. Imagine that the brush/broom is stirring up energy and getting things moving.

Colours

Again think about the colour of things, and how this affects the mood of the place. How do you feel when you are in this room?

Living room

This is the place where you relax. It's the place you come to sit down and rest after a hard day at work. It's a place where everyone can sit together and chat. It's also the place where you might find some peace, so it's important that this room feels safe and comfortable.

Furnishings

As mentioned in Chapter 2, you can turn your coffee table into an altar. Think about the different things that you might want to put on it; things that look attractive but also have a purpose. Include crystals and stones of significance, pictures that create the right kind of mood or feeling, photographs of loved ones (as they are part of you and what is important in your life). Always keep a vase of fresh flowers on your coffee table; in fact you can fill your living room with flowers and plants to encourage nurturing feelings.

Bedroom

The bedroom is the place you go to rest, the safe haven at the end of a long and weary day. We spend a lot of time in the bedroom, although for most of it we are asleep. It is the place we go to dream, the place where dreams come true, and also where we create romance and passion. As with all the other rooms of your house, you can decorate it with these things in mind.

Accessories

Crystals are wonderful bedroom accessories: not only do they look pretty, they can be charged with a particular purpose. Dreaming crystals can be placed around the bed and on bedside tables, rose quartz can be charged to encourage the flow of love and romance, amethyst can be charged to stimulate healing and relaxing energies.

Make up some pot pourri using oils, herbs and rose petals. Not only will it give the room a lovely scent, it will enhance the atmosphere.

Dream catchers are often hung on bedroom walls above the head of the bed. Native Americans believed that the catcher would capture your dreams, getting rid of harmful, negative ones, and keeping the good ones to be enjoyed and remembered. They are an attractive accessory and will encourage you to remember your dreams, which has to be a good thing!

I have mentioned the use of dream pillows before, and dreaming is an excellent time for the subconscious to seek magical solutions to problems and to carry out spells. If there's a particular spell that you have been working on over a period of days, remember to take it to bed with you. Not literally of course: I wouldn't recommend leaving candles or oils burning over night. What you can do is take the ingredients from the spell and place them underneath your bed. Say a few words before you go to sleep and trust that the magic works in your subconscious during the night.

Furnishings

Bedrooms are probably one of the most romantic and relaxing rooms in the house, so treat them as such. Ban televisions, stereos and computers. This is not a room that needs distractions, and these electrical appliances will only drain your energies. If you have problems sleeping, try not to eat or drink in the bedroom, as this distracts from the main purpose of the room. The brain is easily tricked into patterns of behaviour, so you need to constantly reaffirm that this room is the place where you go to rest and regenerate every day. Keep things simple and uncluttered.

Colours
Good colours for bedrooms are soft blues, greens, pinks and creams. Loud colours encourage action and activity; soft, pale colours are soothing and relaxing.

Study/office
I include this room because many people tend to bring work home with them and even for those that don't, the study becomes an area where they sort things out, use the computer, organise things and generally look to be undisturbed. It's a room where clear thinking is required; a room that should inspire industrious activity, but also a place that is still relaxed enough for creativity to flow.

Here are some things to bear in mind when decorating your study.

Colours
Light, airy colours help to soothe the mind and keep it open. Green is good for creativity, as are white and lemon shades. If you need lots of mental stimulation, orange is a good colour: it's bright and cheerful and will encourage activity.

Accessories
Keep fresh plants or flowers in your study to promote the growth of

ideas. Yellow and white flowers in particular will give an air of peace and positivity. A pot of rosemary on your desk will help to keep you alert and on the ball.

The scent of fresh coffee stimulates hard work and effort, so keep some coffee on the boil, or try coffee-scented candles.

This is common sense, but our thoughts have a direct effect on the way we are, how we act and ultimately what we achieve. To condition ourselves to think positively it helps to have reminders dotted about the house. So, stick notes and messages on your walls with inspiring sentences and affirmations.

More advanced magical tools

Magical tools are everywhere, from the mirror to the cooking pot; we have them at our fingertips. There are, however, less everyday tools that can be used in magical work that you might want to investigate further.

Images

Images are very important in magic, whether they are the images we picture in our minds as we perform a spell, or an image that we place on our altar or sacred space. Images symbolise emotions. They resonate with our needs.

If you have children, think about a picture your child has drawn for you. It is powerful because of what it represents, because of the love and effort behind it. You proudly display it on your kitchen wall for all to see. It is a symbol of the bond between mother and child. It is magic in its purest sense because it celebrates your relationship and keeps that special bond strong.

The tarot

Some of the most powerful images in the world can be found in the tarot.

Some people shy away from tarot reading because they feel it has evil connotations. This is not true. The tarot is a tool like anything else. It can be used to show us how things will be if we follow a particular route. There is always an element of choice, and nothing is set in stone. It is best to think of the tarot as a friend, a personal advisor. It offers help and advice when requested. The tarot is not there to scare us.

The images of the Major Arcana are very powerful. These are the cards which are not part of the four suits (cups, wands, coins, swords). These cards have a strong influence on our lives. Invest in a good reference book and learn the meanings of the Major Arcana. Spend time looking at the cards and thinking about what each picture means to you. What feelings does it stir? When you have enough information and insight you can use the cards in your magical work. I suggest having two packs of cards, one for divination and one for spells.

Legal aid

Justice is an excellent card to use in any spells concerned with the law and legal proceedings. If you have a court case coming up, or some sort of legal wrangling, try this spell.

On a Tuesday, light a white candle while visualising your aim. You can burn some cinnamon oil for success. Take the Justice card and write your magical need upon it. Say the following words, or something similar:

Justice be fair. Justice be true.
The outcome is favourable.
I ask this through you.
So mote it be.

Then burn the card in the flame. When you have done this, collect up all the ashes and keep them in a pouch as a charm to help you on the day of your hearing or court case.

Sometimes, focusing on a card's image while thinking about your magical aim is enough. You may also choose to use the cards in guided visualisations. For example, the Sun is a lovely warm card to use for rejuvenation. Imagine yourself stepping into the card; see the colours and feel the texture of your surroundings. Take a moment to drink in those emotions and really feel the Sun warming your heart and soul.

Don't be afraid to use cards that might at first appear scary. Death does not mean death in the tarot. It represents a period of rebirth, moving on to a new cycle in your life. If you are going through a period of change, spend some time in visualisation with the Death card. It will help you move on into the unknown with confidence.

Spend as much time as you like experimenting with the images of the tarot. You will learn much about yourself and others through this wonderful tool.

Runes and ogham stones

Another magical tool to use is the set of runes. These are ancient symbols that have been inscribed into stone or wood. Runes can be used to predict future events or influences by casting them upon the floor. They are read depending on the way they fall and the symbols chosen. The symbols can be used in magic spells, carried in charm bags, or worn as jewellery to imbue the wearer with a specific energy. Celtic ogham stones are very similar. Look into symbols around the world. You can use any symbol or image in your magical work.

Astrology

Most people know what star sign they are. The astrological

influences upon people and things are very important when it comes to working spells. There are certain times and phases when the planets are aligned (or not) when it is better to perform a certain spell. You don't have to become an expert in astrology to find this out: many books have this basic information, and so does the internet. It helps to be aware of the planets as they move through the cosmos.

Numerology

Don't underestimate the power of numbers. Mathematical systems have been around since the beginning of time and underpin the fabric of our society. Numerology is the study of numbers relating to our birth dates and names. It suggests that these numbers are significant to our destiny. Everything on this planet has a number. You can work out an item's specific number to find out what its power is and how it can be used in magic.

It's an interesting exercise to find out your own destiny number, and it may help to explain why we are drawn to certain numbers, houses, areas and so on. To work out your destiny number, first take your date of birth and reduce it to number form:

10 May 1972 becomes 10/05/1972.

Next add the individual digits together: 1 + 0 + 0 + 5 + 1 + 9 + 7 + 2 = 25.

Now add further to reduce the number down to a single number: 2 + 5 = 7.

So, the destiny number is 7.

Any good book on numerology will tell you the significance of the numbers and the various life-paths associated with them.

Psychic development

As explained earlier, as you develop magically, so you will develop psychically. The two processes are interlinked, for you cannot use magic without developing an awareness of the psychic world. So, it also makes sense that any psychic exercises you do will help to strengthen your magic.

Don't panic! Psychic exercise does not involve great physical feats, although you may feel quite tired when you have finished. You can exercise your psychic muscle any time and anywhere.

Auras

In magic, we attribute certain powers with things. Every living thing has an aura. The following exercise will help you to see the aura of a person or object. It will also strengthen your psychic muscles.

Make sure you have plenty of time and space to yourself, so unhook the phone, send the family out, and don't answer the door. You may wish to start this exercise with a visualisation to calm and clear the mind. You may want to invoke your Inner Goddess to tap into your inner power in preparation.

You can do this exercise with any object, but I suggest a piece of fruit like an apple, as it's mobile and of a size that makes it easy to focus on.

Place the apple on the floor in front of you. Look at it closely for a minute or two, just as you would if you were practising visualisation. Notice the shape and size, the colour and contours of the fruit. Notice everything you can about this apple.

Now close your eyes. Bring the apple to your mind's eye. See the image as if it's being flashed on a big screen. Now imagine that the apple has a light surrounding it. What colour is that light? Is it thick or thin? Does it flash different colours and shapes? This is the energy field of the apple. This is the specific energy of the fruit.

Now take a breath, take your time and open your eyes. Look at the apple once more, but this time don't strain or examine it too much. Let your eyes relax. Let your eyelids drop a little, almost as if you are losing focus. Note what you see. Can you see the aura, and, if so, what colour is it?

Don't try too hard. If you can't see anything, don't worry. This is a skill that takes time to develop. Repeat this exercise at regular intervals and try it with different things; other fruits or vegetables, crystals or stones, plants, flowers and people.

Once you can see the aura of an object you can imbue that object with extra power. This is particularly useful when preparing and charging meals and helps you get the most out of your food, and spells!

Dreams

As mentioned in Chapter 13, as you develop (magically and psychically) you will find that your dreams become more vivid and you recall them easily. It's a good idea to keep a dream diary and write down any impressions you have. Although a number of good books on dream meanings are available, the best interpretations will be the ones you come up with yourself.

Witchy words of wisdom

This book has given you the basics that you need for a little everyday witchcraft. It has showed you that most of the tools and ingredients are things you use on a daily basis; it has demonstrated techniques to develop your magical powers and simple spells which can be tailored to suit your needs. Everything in this book can be incorporated into a busy lifestyle, turning you into a house witch as well as a housewife and an all-round modern enchantress!

Be careful what you wish for

Remember to respect the knowledge and the craft. The key with any magic (as with anything in life) is that what you put in will return to you. In other words, be careful what you wish for. Make sure you have thought long and hard about your needs and your motives. Always question why you want something, and work towards making it for the greater good, rather than ultimately selfish reasons.

Magic is not a tool to be abused. It should never be used to manipulate others. Spells that are used in this way always backfire. As long as you maintain a good heart, there is nothing to worry about.

Respect the nature of all things: plants, animals, stones, trees and of course people! Appreciate the Earth and your surroundings. Nurture Mother Nature and she will nurture you. Remember, a casual stroll in the park can be a magical experience; a time for clearing your mind, visualising goals and tapping into the magnificence of the landscape.

Enjoy!

Have fun experimenting with spells. Nothing is carved in stone and you will discover your own path. Follow your instincts. As you learn to listen to your Inner Goddess, things will fall into place. You may be looking to solve a problem, or searching for a herb to soothe a particular physical ailment, and the answer will come in the form of book lent to you by a friend, or a picture in a dream. This synchronicity is not just a coincidence, it's a magical gift.

Magic opens doors and worlds; it makes you appreciate the beauty of life and also the beauty within. So what are you waiting for? Embrace your sexy sorceress self and let the enchantment begin!

Bibliography and further reading

Bibliography

Judika Illes, *The Element Encyclopedia of 5000 Spells*, Element Books, 2004

HE Wedeck, *The Dictionary of Magic*, Philosophical Library, 1973 .

Scott Cunningham, *Cunningham's Encyclopedia of Wicca in the Kitchen*, Llewellyn Publications, 2003

Scott Cunningham, *Cunningham's Encyclopedia of Magical Herbs*, Llewellyn Publications, 2005

Julia Morton, *Herbs and Spices*, Golden Press, 1976

Suggested reading

For more information on the Wiccan path and magic in general, I thoroughly recommend any book by Scott Cunningham, an incredible witch and a great inspiration. The following is a short reading list to help you on your way, all produced by Llewellyn Publications.

Cunningham's Encyclopedia of Wicca in the Kitchen

Cunningham's Encyclopedia of Magical Herbs

Cunningham's Encyclopedia of Crystal, Gem and Metal Magic

Index

alters, 27
astrological associations, 40
auras, 172

baby charm, 91
balance, 16
belief, 20
broom, 58

candle magic, 35, 78
charms, 36
circle, 27
coffee-table alters, 28

dream pillows, 34
dreams, 173

elementals, 71
erotic dreams, 156

fertility salad, 89
festivals, 41
flying, 30

gambling charm, 99
goddesses, 61

Halloween, 41, 42
healing hands,144
heartache, 83
herbs, 46

images, 168
inner goddess, 21-2
intention, 19
invisibility spell, 141

legal aid, 169
love bath, 78

magic, 18
magical baths, 34
magical marriage, 86
magical mirror, 138
mirror, 58
modern magic, 8

personal courage, 127
personal protection juice, 135
power oil. 125
protection techniques, 29
psychic development, 171
psychic dream pillow, 155
psychology, 29

ritual, 21
rosemary, 94, 107, 109, 123, 124

salad supper, 150
saliva, 123
sore throat, 115
spell boxes, 59
spells, 33, 34, 36, 44
spirit guides, 69
stress, 119
success wish, 98

tea tree oil, 113
thinking ahead, 25

viruses, 119
vitality, 121

wand, 57
wheel of fortune, 101
wishing spells, 143